18th Century
DÉCOUPAGE

The Definitive Guide

MILNER CRAFT SERIES

18th Century
DÉCOUPAGE

The Definitive Guide

First published in 1994 by
Sally Milner Publishing Pty Ltd
558 Darling Street
Rozelle NSW 2039
Australia

© Val Lade 1994

Cover & colour design by Stan Lamond, Lamond Art & Design
Photography by Neil Lorimer
Typesetting by Emsee Publishing Design
Printed in Australia by Pirie Printers

National Library of Australia
Cataloguing-in-Publication data:

Lade, Val.
    18th century decoupage.

    ISBN 1 86351 133 4.

    1. Decoupage. 2. Decoupage -History - 18th century
    I. Title. II. Title: Eighteenth century decoupage. (Series:
    Milner craft series)

745.546.

To Nerida Singleton, without whose gentle,
persuasive encouragement this book
would not have been written.

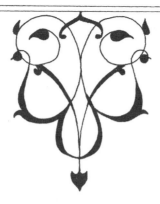

CONTENTS

INTRODUCTION

'If you can create something time cannot erode, something which ignores the eccentricities of particular eras or moments, something truly timeless, this is the ultimate victory.' Although I don't know who wrote these words, they had an impact on my life that I hope is reflected in my work. Perhaps of all the decorative arts découpage is the most timeless. Over the past 15 years, many exponents of the art have produced beautiful work, which I know will be as treasured in a 100 years as it is today.

How can I explain the passion I have for découpage? It has taken over my life to the point where I no longer teach painting and rarely tackle a canvas any more. In the mid-1970s, I was at the home of the well-known fibre artist Sue Trytell, where she was working on one of her huge wall hangings. As a painter, I was fascinated by the line and texture of her work. She showed me some découpage illustrations in an American magazine and said: 'Val, learn to do this and teach it, for I feel it is right for you'.

I began to research découpage and the more I learnt, the more fascinating it became. I read everything I could find on the subject and began experimenting, but I soon realised that Australia's climatic conditions meant that the materials used, for instance, in the USA were not suitable. Most brands of lacquers that were available at that time could not withstand the sudden temperature changes that Melbourne experiences.

To hamper my progress, I was also on my own. It seemed that nobody in Australia had heard of découpage. Frustration followed, but eventually I had incredibly good fortune. Two people became very interested in the technical challenge that I was presenting them: Richard Bell of Wattyl

Paints and Lacquers and Philip Dawson, an abrasives expert. I had known Richard for a whole year before he confessed to me that he had invented Estapol while a young chemist with Wattyl and he could not believe the stress I was putting on his product. Philip drew on his wide knowledge of abrasives and came up with sandpapers and grits I'd never discovered in any hardware store. In turn, Richard was fascinated with the abrasives I was using on his product.

After a year's hard slog, I gave the very first class at the Caulfield Arts Centre in 1977, following it soon after with others at the Council of Adult Education. I have since introduced découpage to hundreds of people. Teaching and producing découpage and helping other tutors to get started has kept me so busy that I pushed the idea of a book to the dim recesses of my mind. Nerida Singleton took some months to convince me that there were people out there who really needed my knowledge and so I began – with awe – to sort out the knowledge I had gained over so many years. I can only hope that you will find it informative and valuable. For some, it will introduce an art form that is absorbing and special, while others will be encouraged to explore new methods with their work.

Hiram Manning wrote of découpage: 'people enjoy a renaissance of spirit'. This is, without question, true. It brings another dimension to one's life – one of sheer delight. I have always shared every scrap of my hard-won knowledge verbally; it now seems time to write it down.

A BRIEF HISTORY OF DÉCOUPAGE

It appears that découpage originated in Venice in the 1750s, where it was known as *lacca povera* (poor man's lacquer) or *l'arte del povero* (the poor man's art). At that time the artists of the day simply could not keep up with the demand for lacquered work. Several firms of printers, but principally the Remondini family of Bassano, produced sheets of engravings specially for *lacca povera* decoration. These were coloured, cut, designed and pasted onto prepared surfaces, then varnished many times to resemble the high gloss of lacquer decoration on items such as desks, chairs, tables, cabinets and screens. Each of these stages in the process was allocated to a level of craftsman in the Guild system.

At the height of its popularity, *lacca povera* was produced in other Italian cities and it spread throughout Europe. France gave it the name of 'découpage' (from *découper* to cut) and Marie Antoinette and the ladies of the Court became so enthusiastic that they cut up everything in sight in pursuit of the art. It is said that original works of Boucher and Watteau were not safe from these ladies' scissors!

In England at this time there lived a Mary Delany. At the age of 73 she began to cut exquisite flowers from coloured papers that she had specially made. The pictures that she made were accurate and exact in every detail and without doubt, her cuttings remain unsurpassed. They may be seen in the British Museum. *Mrs Delany Her Life And Her Flowers* by Ruth Hayden (published by Colonade Books, British Museum Publications Ltd) illustrates her remarkable work.

Later on, Queen Victoria became not only a découpeur but also a collector of découpage. During Victorian times, fashionable young ladies often executed a screen as part of their trousseau. Using a black background, sources from the *Ladies Amusements Book* and *Godey's Lady's Book* were glued and varnished. Often small family likenesses were inserted in the design. I have seen several of these screens in England's stately homes, while others exist in private family collections in Melbourne.

The vogue for découpage faded in England around the time of the outbreak of the First World War, when the lifestyle of the English changed dramatically. In France, découpage ceased with the French Revolution, while in Venice, the very heart of its beginning, no découpage of any note has been produced since Napoleon marched into that city.

Last September, the Palladio Foundation in Melbourne arranged for me to do research in Venice into what had happened to this fine art. Dr Romano Toppan and Dr Wolfdietrich Elbert of the European Centre for Training Craftsmen in the Conservation of the Architectural Heritage, told me that in Venice découpage is practically extinct. Vittorio Biasotto, Venice's most eminent artisan, took me on a tour of the few remaining expert lacquer studios. Each of these craftsmen had learnt their lacquering skills from previous generations of their family. Their studios were piled high with restoration work waiting to be done. The shellac on découpage furniture and boxes had become badly crazed. There appeared to be enough restoration work for a 100 years. Vittorio explained that skilled lacquerers were few and their restoration work never-ending. All three men agreed that the Venetians of today would not be prepared to tackle such a time-consuming skill.

They were truly enchanted with the pieces I took to give them, but their culture is so locked into tradition and the methods of the Renaissance, that modern paints and lacquers are abhorrent to them. The Venetians, who created this beautiful art form, introduced so many innovations and produced it with such joy for so many decades, cannot contemplate an approach using modern materials. It is a sad loss for, I think, no other people have such style and elegance in design as the

Italians – a tradition that goes back to Etruscan times.

When Hiram Manning discovered découpage in the home of some descendants of the craft guildsmen in France before the Second World War, he and his mother became fascinated with the art form and its formulae and techniques. After the war, they began to teach it in the United State of America, adding their own techniques and variations. It appealed to all age groups and eventually a national Guild of Découpeurs was formed.

I have been teaching découpage in Australia since 1977 in Melbourne and the Découpage Guild Australia Inc. was established in 1984 (the address is PO Box 395, Malvern 3144). We have been fortunate indeed that this fine art has been able to develop in Australia without any rigid outside influences; perhaps this is because we are isolated geographically and are a young country. We learn from traditional methods and styles but feel free to adapt them to our own style and introduce our own innovations. We are indeed 'the lucky country' in this respect.

TECHNIQUES

This section presents all the technical information you will need on découpage, including some design considerations. It is important that you read this part thoroughly before embarking on any project.

PREPARING SURFACES

Any hard surface can be used for découpage; for example, wood, bisque, glazed pottery, glass, stone, driftwood, metal, marble, plastic (provided it is rigid), iron, egg shells, even cement. The possibilities are simply endless. The preparation for any surface not specified here should be tackled with common sense; for example, a cement tub would need much heavy sanding, a coat or two of gesso and a sealant.

GESSO

The surface of wood has been used by artists to paint on for many centuries. During the fifteenth century, canvas gradually replaced wood as the base of most paintings, but a ground still had to be applied to each of these surfaces, and this ground was gesso. The essential elements of gesso were (and still are) an inert filler and a binder. It is important to use a good quality gesso (such as Liquitex) to avoid cracking problems.

Much has been said about using gesso as a preparation and many people plaster it on with gay abandon, without understanding its use and disregarding its cost.

To put it simply; you need to use gesso in the following cases.

- To prepare a styrene foam ball. First sand the ball very lightly with No. 320# stearate sandpaper to remove any ridges. Two or three coats of gesso will help disguise the texture, mask manufacturing faults and strengthen it.

- To prepare on an egg shell that is slightly greasy. Sometimes duck eggs are greasy, but paint goes on most shells easily. Certainly an emu or ostrich egg will benefit from several layers of gesso as their texture is unattractive.

- On anything old you have restored or when the woodgrain on a box is indented or scoured. Deep imperfections can be disguised with a mixture of Polyfilla and a polymer medium such as Liquitex Gloss Medium and Varnish. Just mix these to a stiff paste and apply with a palette knife. Sand the surface smooth when it is dry.

- When you are working on glass or glazed objects. As acrylic paints don't adhere well to these surfaces, first apply gesso and allow it to dry. Lacquer the gesso before painting. The lacquer will protect the gesso from becoming moist and falling away from the surface when paint is applied. Paint adheres quite well to lacquer.

- Several coats of gesso, sanded smooth, make an excellent white background if you plan to have a series of water glazes. They will give a luminosity to the washes.

It is not necessary to use gesso in the following cases.

- When you are working on clean, freshly fired bisque. However, occasionally you might strike a small patch that refuses to take paint. This is caused by the oil in the fingers of the potter as he handled the work during manufacture. Simply apply a small amount of gesso to this area and, when dry, proceed with the paint.

- When you are using clean, smooth terracotta.

- When you are using woodwork with a smooth, sanded surface.

- When you are using new craftwood. However, craftwood has a formaldehyde content and it is best sealed with Gloss Medium and Varnish.

- When you are using most hen and goose eggs. Give them a good scrub with scouring powder before or after blowing.

Always ask yourself why you are applying something and if you can't come up with a reason, don't do it.

WOODEN SURFACES

A piece of découpage takes many weeks to complete, so it is important that you take time to prepare the article that you will be working on well. I am by nature a thoroughly impatient person and had to really take myself in hand over this issue. Below are a few basic pointers.

1. Remove, if possible, all catches and hinges whether they are rusty or not. When boxes are made specially for découpage, they come without fittings or the hinges come separately, for lacquering around hinges is difficult.

2. If you are working on an old box or tray, there are two ways you can go.

- If the wood is painted or lacquered and in good condition with no lumps, bumps or ridges, you may feel the task of stripping it is a great deal of trouble. Provided it is in excellent condition, all you need to do is seal off the current paint and/or lacquer from your own work. Apply a coat of polymer medium and leave it to dry for several hours. Then apply two coats of Estapol lacquer, allowing 24 hours drying time in between the coats. This will effectively seal off any paint or lacquer which may not agree chemically with the materials you are using. Depending on the colour your background is to be, you may need to apply a coat of gesso. If your background colour is dark, this will not be necessary.

- If the wood is in poor condition and the paint or lacquer is peeling off, I'm afraid that stripping it right back is the only solution.

3. Should you contemplate working on one of the imported wooden salad bowls that abounded in the 1950s, you will need to seal the surface completely for these bowls were heavily oiled. Use the same technique as for wood in good condition, explained in point 2 above.

4. If you have re-stained an old table or cabinet and wish to use it for découpage, apply a coat of lacquer to seal the stain before gluing prints. In fact, if you are in doubt about any old surface, seal it first rather than have your work spoiled.

POROUS SURFACES

The two most porous surfaces to be aware of are terracotta and egg shells.

TERRACOTTA

Before working on terracotta, seal off the inside and outside with two coats of lacquer, allowing each coat 24 hours to dry, before commencing work.

EGG SHELLS

I learnt about the high porosity of egg shells the hard way. Having just completed a goose egg as a diplomatic gift to Japan, I sat it on the dining table to await packaging. The design had ibis on the wing, with a copper and burnt-umber background and it was touched with gold. A couple of days later as I passed the egg, my affectionate gaze froze to horror, for it definitely looked peculiar. The piece seemed to have acquired a faint green tinge and part of the design looked slightly raised. I forced myself to think coherently, for this was Monday and the gift was to fly to Japan on the following Friday. Logically, the cause had to be moisture and as none could possibly penetrate through the layers of Estapol lacquer, it had to be from inside. The tiny hole at the base, which had been sealed, had to be re-opened. Two wee drops of moisture fell out. During either the wet-and-dry sanding or the micromesh process, water had entered the egg, which had then been sealed with the water inside. The water had a splendid time working its way through the shell. I sat for a whole evening with a hair drier blowing warm air through the hole. The raised design returned to normal, as did most of the paint colour, but I left it until the last moment to reseal the end. I am now extra careful when working with eggs and never seal them until a week after finishing. It is most important to seal off the egg finally so that no moisture can enter the hole after the egg has left your care.

CUTTING

Fine, excellent cutting is vital to découpage, without it you will have poor découpage. Nothing can really disguise poor cutting. It is the very essence of your work and the heart of découpage, therefore it is important to have the right scissors. With poor scissors, you will find it difficult to achieve fine work. Most good scissors are made in Germany and are of high quality steel. The best ones are manufactured for surgical cutting of the iris of the eye. They are curved, with fine blades and perfectly sharp, matching points. At the time of the purchase, the points must be examined carefully, I recommend you take a magnifying glass with you. Often tips appear to be pointed but, in fact, may be slightly wedged at the end of one of the blades. A surgical supply company (such as Future Medics) will stock good scissors. Ask for 11.25 cm (4 ½ in) delicate curved, iris scissors. Make sure that the handles are comfortable for your fingers. The length of the scissors overall or the length of the blades is not important and this will vary.

Perfectly matched sharp points   *One point is wedged*

RIGHT   *WRONG*

Experience has taught me that the average person takes about six weeks to learn to cut well. As when you first hold a golf club, cutting with the curved blades of your scissors pointing outwards, away from your hand, may seem strange. However, if you begin the right way, it will soon be natural to hold them this way. There are two important reasons for holding them in this way.

1. The blades slightly bevel the edge of the paper as you cut, which makes gluing easier.

2. You can see more clearly the line along which you are cutting. For instance, you would not wish to cut off the black outline of a delicately coloured fine stem for the image would then disappear into the background paint and be quite lost by the time the varnish is applied.

Firstly, cut the inner areas from behind

In classes, we swap equipment and lend absolutely anything but never our scissors; for, like a fountain pen, each person works the blades into their own particular cutting motion and this may be upset by someone else using them.

Always sit comfortably in a good light when cutting. Consciously relax your shoulder and neck muscles. The cutting arm should rest with the elbow tucked in a relaxed manner into the waist. The only function of this arm and hand is to cut: that is, to open and close the very ends of the blades. If you find that you are tearing the paper and notice the elbow of your cutting arm in the air, start again in the right posture. Hold the scissors with the thumb and forefinger or middle finger, whichever feels most comfortable. The paper is moved with the opposite hand, which guides the paper in and out of the scissors, turning and twisting it as you cut. Right-handers need always to cut in an anti-clockwise direction around the perimeter of the image and clockwise when cutting out inner areas.

Left-handers   *Right-handers*

Left-handers cut clockwise around the perimeter and anti-clockwise for the inner areas.

Once you have the correct scissors, relaxed position and a sensibly sized paper image you are ready to begin. Look carefully at the print and note all the areas that are not accessible to the scissors from the outside. It is vital to cut these inner areas first, while there is still plenty of paper to hold. Using the sharp end of one blade of the scissors, prick a small hole (the size of a pin prick) through the front of the paper in each inner area. Be sure to establish and prick all these areas first. The tiny holes will be very visible from the back of the paper. Hold the scissor blades open and insert the uppermost blade into the hole from the back of the paper. Sometimes you can feel the position while looking at the paper from the front, but if you can't, turn the paper over and the hole you are looking for will be visible. Begin cutting the inner areas from behind, if you are right-handed in a clockwise direction, if you are left-handed, anti-clockwise. If during this process you reach a point where the paper doesn't fit the scissors, remove the blades and cut for as small a way as possible from the top, before returning them below again. After every small inner area is cut, and only then, the cutting of the outer perimeter edges of the design can begin (in an anti-clockwise direction if you are right-handed, clockwise if you are left-handed). If the cutout is particularly complicated with lots of inner areas, beginning to cut out the edges can be a joyful moment for it may have taken some time to cut as many as 50 inner areas!

Use common sense when cutting out. Don't ever feel that you need to cut huge areas at once. Take stock of the shape and content of the design, decide what the largest piece must be and don't exceed that. As you become more skilled with design, it will be unlikely that you will use much of the pattern in original form anyway, but will rearrange the pieces to create your own design.

Some people believe in leaving bridges or narrow strips of paper between fine areas of the design. I can't be bothered with this as I find that even fine paper is strong enough to hold together. Don't worry, however, if you inadvertantly snip off a piece of the design – just put it back in place carefully when you glue. You may even decide not to have that bit in the final design anyway.

Sometimes outlines are indistinct or you may not be sure how much of a design you want. Make a decision and cut the line you want. Remember that you are in charge of your creation and you can cut a fat stem down to the thickness of a cotton thread if you wish.

Take heart when you are just beginning to cut and find you have left some bits of white or other coloured edging. Use a 00 brush and watered-down paint in the appropriate colour to disguise the edging.

I am often asked what part is most difficult to cut well. Tiny butterfly feelers first spring to mind, but actually small circles like blossoms or blue-

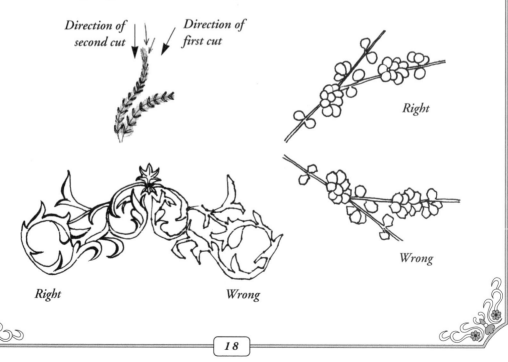

Direction of second cut *Direction of first cut*

Right

Right *Wrong*

Wrong

berries and the inner areas of fine loops are definitely the hardest to manage.

A minute piece of fern is best tackled by feathering the edges. This is done by cutting a series of very fine splits around the edge of the fern in one direction. Then, using a slightly different direction, cut across the outer edges of those splits. This makes the edge uneven and simulates the spiky ends of the fern.

If your cutting out is jagged, the main reason will be that you are not cutting with the very tips of your blades and are opening them out too wide as you cut.

I keep my cutouts on large styrene foam trays. It is easy to catalogue them this way as they can be stacked one upon the other in a drawer. One tray can hold butterflies, another insects, while others can contain Christmas themes, borders, flowers, mediaeval images, and so on. Some designs I cut years ago still lie unused but, one day they will be just what I am seeking.

Cutting is a little like knitting – it can be done in all manner of places. My scissors accompany me on long flights, to football and cricket matches, in parked cars when I waited endlessly for children to emerge from changing rooms, between sets of tennis, on the beach, in the garden – anywhere at all really – and television has to be super interesting to have me rest the scissors down! Over the years, students' husbands have telephoned me, begging me to ban their wives from cutting out in bed. So beware – it becomes an obsession!

If you find you have difficulty seeing what you are cutting when doing particularly fine work, a magnifying glass that hangs around the neck is excellent. They are readily available from opticians.

A word here on painting the edges of cutouts. It is often recommended that you colour the cut edge of the paper. I find this quite unnecessary except when the paper is very thick; for example, a card or photograph. The layers of lacquer will disguise naturally the thinner edges.

Finally, for all those learning this skill, I assure you that you will master cutting out; it is just a matter of practice and time.

DESIGNING

It is little wonder that découpage evolved in Venice, for Italians have an inherent sense of design. It always seems sad to me that in Australia, children, for the most part, are not taught about design at school. They may know what looks right, but have no understanding of why it is so. Therefore, I often find when teaching adults that I must spend time helping them with the basic principles of design: structure, line, form, mass, texture, colour, shade and fitness. In other words, they need to be taught to see these things for themselves before they can apply them to their work. It is only then that they can develop their own style which will make their découpage unique. Developing your own style is important. Think how recognisable Picasso is, no matter which medium he used.

The first – and most obstructive – block to visual learning is the ingrained assumption that only certain things are worth looking at. Look at everything! Try and keep your mind wide open. Guard against attitudes and expectations that can influence you to regard one thing as 'important' and dismiss another.

When you begin découpage much time is spent in mastering its techniques, but along the way, consciously or unconsciously, your style will develop. I could give 12 students the same object upon which to work and the same resources from which to cut, yet 12 totally different designs would emerge. This is the truly wonderful part of découpage – no piece is like any other. While your style is developing, many things will influence you: the work of others around you, work from past eras, experiences from your childhood, all the things that have touched your life and brought beauty into it. Without doubt, artists have always been influenced by the harmony and rhythm of nature. Nothing in nature jars or says: 'Look at me first!'. Dwell on a landscape and your eye may be led to a focal point, such as the autumnal splendour of a liquidambar tree, but it is led gently, for the autumn colours will also be repeated throughout the landscape area. Learn to examine nature, it will be your greatest inspiration.

At the design stage, the cutouts are first applied to the object with blutack, enabling you to change it about, add to or subtract from until the line, space and tonal values of the prints and cutouts are in total harmony with the shape of the object. This is one of the most pleasurable stages of découpage. There are many designs which can be created from one set of resource material that will be right for it. Use your personal creativity to decide what mood you want, what you want to say about the subject matter, what period you want to suggest, and so on. On a practical note, when using blu-tack, roll it into a ball about 4 mm (1/8 in) in diameter and press it gently onto both surfaces. It is worth mentioning here that the quickest way to remove a stray piece of blu-tack is with blu-tack.

There are a number of basic principles that need to be borne in mind and these are as follows.

1. The eye must be allowed to wander.

2. If you have a central theme, the eye should naturally gravitate to that.

3. Space in some areas will emphasise other areas. This space is as important as the design itself.

4. The design should not lead your eye off the object.

5. Your design may be asymmetrical or symmetrical depending on your subject matter. Do not attempt asymmetry if your object has a symmetrical shape; for example, a hexagonal, lidded urn. If you are working with a round, free-flowing shape and your design is asymmetrical, then space becomes even more important.

Wrong 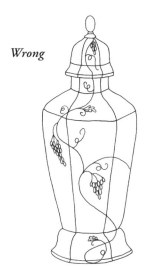    *Right*

An asymmetrical approach is unsuitable for this structured shape

6. If you have a central theme, make certain the design around it marries with it in colour, tone and size. It is often successful to select small areas of colour or content from the central theme. For instance, if your central theme is a beautiful lady in a garden (see colour plate) select the soft red of the butterfly and hair garland and repeat it in the surrounding design.

It is vital that the design cutouts are sympathetic to the central theme. Where you have a delicate watercolour print as the main theme, do not use cutouts in the rest of design that have been executed in a heavy style in oil paint. Similarly, do not use an untonal woodblock print with a richly painted Rembrandt print.

7. If the shape on which you are working is irregular; for example, an elegant, lidded urn that is wide at the top and gradually tapers to a thinner base, your design must respect the shape and the larger areas of the design should be confined to the wider area. Otherwise, the balance of the object will be upset and the eye would be led off the piece.

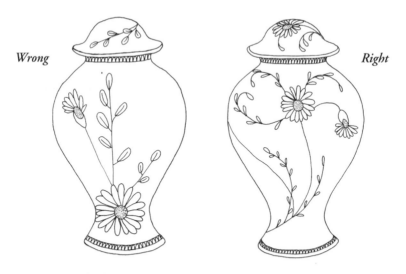

The design of the left-hand urn leads the eye right off the base

Bearing all these points in mind, begin by placing your main image in position. It may be a print or a design shape. Then work around the main image.

If you are working on a round box, for example, begin with the lid.

Keep to the round shape of the box, even if you use a sparse design. Next, tackle the sides. Blu-tack on a small area of design. If it pleases you, you can repeat it:

- on the opposite side
- at measured quarterly intervals
- continuously around
- in an asymmetrical sweep, even up and over the lid.

Some possible arrangements for cutouts

A basic lesson in marrying shapes is to consider how you can arrange an oblong and an oval. The diagrams below show an arrangement that works and one that does not.

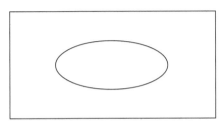

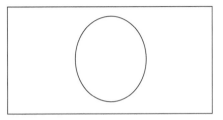

Right

Wrong

The shapes are in harmony & balance

The oval opposes the rectangle

Another point to consider is the tonal value of the elements of the design. Tones are the varying shades of one colour. A child will often colour a tree trunk plain brown. This, of course, is not true to nature at all. Far from it. Look at tree trunks and you will find varying tones of three or four different colours, all in harmony. Therefore, if your main theme has an abundance of scarlet or cadmium red (both yellow-based reds), you should not use cutouts in crimsons or violets (blue-based reds). It would not be harmonious. With scarlet or cadmium red you could introduce pinks, but only those with an underlying yellow tone; for example, the pink tone of a Lorraine Lee rose would be wrong, but a pale apricot rose would be fine. If you are in doubt about a colour, a good way to test it is to mix the colour of the main theme on a palette and then make it lighter by adding white. If your cutout doesn't look the same as the shade you have mixed, it is wrong. It can be lighter or darker than the shade, but not a different hue.

Never be influenced by the existing design of the resource material. You must shape it and make it work for you. As you become more skilled, you may use up to a dozen different sources to make your own design. This is the most challenging part of découpage. Remember that you are the artist and make your resources work for you, regardless of how they were originally presented.

My advice is to blu-tack the cutouts on and, when you are satisfied, 'live with' the design for a few hours, looking at it from all angles until you are sure you really like it. I live with my designs for several days sometimes, as I like to see them in both day and night light.

If you find, on looking at a design over some time, that something appears not to be right, but you can't determine just what is wrong, try one of the following tricks.

1. Place it in front of a mirror and look at its reflection. The reverse image often shows up a poor line or tone.

2. Look at it with dark sunglasses on. You may then see a tone among the cutouts that is too dominant or not strong enough.

3. Almost close your eyes and look at your project. A glaring error of tone will be immediately evident, or something might say: 'look at me first'.

4. As you are working, always stand well back from your work and look at it with the surrounding area shut off. You can do this by cutting a postage-stamp-sized hole in a postcard to look through, but I always make a vision tunnel with an almost closed fist. It is amazing how different it appears when your eye is not distracted by surrounding images.

There are very few rigid rules in découpage, but the following is one of them: never decide on the colour of your painted background until your design has been blue-tacked on the object. To paint it first and then try to accomodate that paint colour with design tones is the most frustrating exercise you could give yourself.

Lastly, designing découpage can be subtle or bold, modern or traditional but it must always preserve harmony of shape and tonal value to be effective.

PAINTING

Acrylic paints are the most suitable for découpage. They dry quickly and remain stable in changing climatic conditions. They can be thinned with polymer medium or water. These paints dry quickly because the chemical structure has a porosity that allows complete evaporation to occur. They have strong adhesion and each layer binds itself well to the one underneath. Research also suggests that they are resistant to oxidising and chemical breakdown.

CARE OF PAINTS

When you squeeze paint from a tube a certain amount collects around the nozzle. This paint hardens and so the cap will not fit back exactly again. Air can then infiltrate the paint causing it to either harden or liquify. To avoid this, keep the nozzle clean and wipe any excess paint from it with a soft rag.

CARE OF BRUSHES AND SPONGES

Brushes may be sable, synthetic or bristle. Sponges may be synthetic or natural sea sponge. Acrylic paint dries very quickly, so good care must be taken of all of your tools. As soon as you have finished painting, wash your brush or sponge in water very thoroughly, working out every bit of remaining paint. Squeeze the last of the rinsing water out and leave them to dry. In the case of a brush, lightly form the bristles back into their true shape and stand them with the bristles pointing upward. Do not use hot water on sea sponges as it will cause them to shrivel and matt.

If paint has dried rock hard on your brush or sponge, soak it for 12 hours in methylated spirits, then work the paint out with your fingers. If this does not work, leave it for 15 minutes in cheap nail varnish remover. In both cases, finally wash it well with warm soapy water and rinse with cold water until all the soap residue is removed, then dry. As I do not always practise what I preach, I have had dried paint disasters and have rescued the brush, but it is never quite the same after being subjected to this treatment.

PALETTE

The simplest palette is a white ice-cream carton lid. This is ideal as it is flat, takes a number of colours and allows you to move your brush or sponge around it. Never use a watercolour palette with little compartments for the paints – it is too restrictive and you need a flat surface.

You can also 'store' paint on the lid. To do this, put a small piece of wet sponge in the ice-cream carton and replace the lid, with the paint still on it, on the carton and the paint will keep moist for days. This makes an economical 'wet palette' and saves wastage. The paint doesn't seem to fall off the lid.

An old white plate can be used as a palette also. In this case, if you wish to save paint, place a thoroughly wetted piece of sponge on the plate beside the paint to be saved and cover the plate with plasticwrap or foil.

If you are not saving paint in this manner, always clean your palette thoroughly. Do not put fresh paint over old paint that has set. The moisture will eventually cause it to flake off and spoil the colour of your new paint.

BUYING PAINTS

There are several brands of acrylic paints on the market that work well for découpage. In class we mainly use Liquitex, Atelier (artist quality) and Matisse. Liquitex is the 'Rolls Royce' of acrylic paints and the brand I personally use. Since they are manufactured in the USA, they are more expensive, but the pigments remain true, the texture of the paint is consistent and the skilfully designed tube and cap prevent changes within. You can squeeze the last drop from the tube and it will be as fresh as it was when opened.

Below are some colours that I recommend that you buy. You will notice that I have specified the iridescent ones be Liquitex as the iridescent colours are unique. Some other brands do have iridescent shades – Windsor and Newton have a good 'wedding band' gold and there are a few other golds on the market, but I find they resemble bronze more than gold. If you have the four Liquitex iridescent shades, you can mix any iridescent colour you wish.

Liquitex

Iridescent gold
Iridescent copper
Iridescent white
Iridescent bronze

Liquitex, Atelier (artist quality), Matisse

Titanium white	Mars black
Cadmium red medium	Crimson
Acra violet	Cadmium yellow medium
Cobalt blue	Yellow ochre
Ultramarine blue	Burnt umber
Phthalocyanine blue	Burnt sienna
Hookers green (pure, not hookers green hue)	
Phthalocyanine green	Dioxine purple

Most art supply shops will give a 10 per cent discount to students if you produce a receipt from your class. Naturally, you don't need to buy all the above colours at once. If you are just starting out, begin with the primary colours, which will give you a good range of tones. If anyone asks me what I would like for my birthday or Christmas, I always ask for paints!

SELECTING THE BACKGROUND COLOUR

For me, background colour is everything. It is the very soul of your découpage. Having said that, let me state firmly that painting is neither difficult nor a mystery. It truly doesn't matter if the last tube of paint you opened was in Grade 6, or the best you ever did was colour in with a box of watercolours. It's immaterial, for a whole new world awaits you.

As you consider what colours you feel may look good behind your cutout design, it is important to keep some things in mind.

1. Do you want the cutouts to disappear into or become part of the background?

2. Do you want a contrast to your cutouts so that their fine cutting will be highlighted?

3. Do you want to suggest a rough or smooth texture?

4. Do you want a rhythm in the painting to complement the rhythm of your design?

5. Do you want to suggest sunlight, moonlight, winter, summer, movement, tranquillity, space, richness, delicacy, depth, translucency, strength, and so on?

6. Do you want to emphasise a tiny tone within your design or blend the major tone of your image over the whole piece?

Your choice is what will help make your work unique. If you are working with a design and shape you really love (and I think it is important to do this) then the painted background will fall into place for you because you will visualise the piece as a whole.

There are no rules for putting on the paint – you can use anything from a brush or sponge to your finger tip or a rag. However, the one rule upon which I insist when teaching is that colours are never mixed on the palette but directly on the background surface. Pre-mixing a colour on the palette is the quickest route to muddied shades that I know and, frankly, you may as well just go to the hardware store and buy a pot of paint in that particular colour.

APPLYING THE PAINT

Before beginning, have a fresh jar of water to hand, and replace it as soon as it gets murky.

When you are experimenting do not have too many colours on your palette – it's not only unnecessary but can actually be confusing. Moisten your brush or sponge a little and, above all, be generous with the amount of paint you place on your palette. There is nothing worse than when you are applying the paint in a rhythm to have to stop and squeeze out more from the tube.

Learn to apply paint quickly and confidently as this is the key to success. Know when to stop – don't overwork the background and paint out an effect with which you were happy.

Just some of the effects you can get with paint are given below.

Opaque: Apply undiluted paint to give a solid colour.

Glazing: Work transparent layers of paint over an opaque paint. A luminosity and depth are produced when the opaque colour underneath shows through the transparent glaze. It gives a three-dimensional quality.

Wet into wet: Work two or three colours into each other at once to give an illusion of depth and dimension. This is especially effective if worked over a dried background of yet another colour.

Frottage: A patch of heavy, opaque colour is worked over another dried opaque colour. It is then covered with a high-gloss paper, which is rubbed and carefully removed to give an irregular texture.

Unpainted areas: Use masking tape, a sticky brown tape, to cover an area you wish to remain unpainted. It pulls off easily when the paint is dry, leaving a clean border line.

Scumbling: Paint the background and allow to dry. Using a stiff, wedged brush and very little paint, work quickly and firmly over the surface in another colour at random. Use a circular motion and allow much of the original colour to show through. You can also get this effect by applying the paint in streaks, stipples, finger smudges or dabs.

Hatching: Paint the background and allow to dry. Use either short or long brush strokes to apply the second colour, dragging the brush strokes across each other and leaving some of the colour underneath showing through. This effect can resemble an old tapestry background.

Stippling and splattering: Stippling is applying fine dots to a surface with a brush. Splattering is hitting a brush loaded with watered-down paint against the flat of your hand. Both techniques give shading and texture to the background. Remember to cover with newspaper those areas you don't want splattered.

Marbling: Paint either a light or dark background and let it dry. Load the edge of a wide brush with a contrasting colour mixed half and half with Liquitex Marbling Medium. With the brush in an almost horizontal position, paint wavy lines to look like the veins of marble. To make it more realistic, you can soften the lines with a sponge, rag or paper towel or just work across them with a soft brush. Now use a finer brush and a stronger colour to highlight delicately the existing lines.

I don't expect you to successfully use these techniques all at once, but they are here for when you would like to experiment. The best advice I can give you is to practise with your paints on some white cardboard.

COLOUR

I am not presenting a colour wheel as I feel the best way to learn is to experiment for yourself. You will soon find out, for example:

- cobalt blue and cadmium yellow make green; add a tiny touch of white to cadmium red and you have a perfect Australian bush colour.
- cobalt blue and iridescent gold make a soft green.
- phthalocyanine green used straight from the tube is an ideal Christmas green.
- a mixture of hookers green, copper and gold will give depth to garden greens.

- a mixture of phthalocyanine green, iridescent bronze and iridescent white gives a soft teal green.

The list goes on and on. You can mix absolutely anything you like together (but not on your palette) to achieve a special effect.

The most difficult part is to anticipate how the colour will look under 20 to 30 coats of lacquer. You will learn with experience but, in the meantime, place 20 coats of lacquer on a piece of glass or a glass plate and hold that over the colour. It won't be absolutely accurate, but it will give you an idea. For the most part, colours are magnificently enriched by the coats of Estapol lacquer, but it is best to avoid any pale blues, pinks or mauves. This is because, by covering the paint with Estapol, you are, in fact, adding yellow so pale blues will look more green at the finish, pinks will appear orange and mauves become a rather dirty brown shade that you will hate. If you wish to use these colours, it is wise to use a water-based white lacquer. Naturally, this also applies to a white background that you wish to keep white. If Estapol lacquer is used on a white background it turns to a pleasant, pale biscuit shade, which may or may not be what you want. To help get you started, I am going to give you a list of backgrounds to try. These are all applied with a small, barely moistened sea sponge, as this is very easy to manage. Be sure to use lots of paint.

BACKGROUNDS WITH A BLACK BASE

The following are excellent backgrounds when working with Chinese, Japanese or Middle-Eastern resources as they give an oriental effect, but of course they can be used for other things also.

First paint a plain black opaque background and allow it to dry well.

1. Burnt sienna and iridescent gold.

Pick up some of both these colours together on your sponge and push the sponge down on your palette lightly in order to disperse the paints into the sponge. Gently push the loaded sponge in a slight upward movement over the black background. Lift it off and repeat the process, leaving some of the black showing through. This gives a very rich effect under the lacquer.

2. Acra violet, copper and iridescent gold.

This time collect all three colours on your sponge and use the same technique as for 1 above.

3. Phthalocyanine green and iridescent copper.

Same procedure as for 1 above.

BACKGROUND WITH A BRONZE BASE

Paint the bronze background and allow it to dry well. Use iridescent gold and iridescent copper, working the two colours together as in 1 above. Let some of the bronze show through.

The backgrounds above will give a textured effect to your work. This may not be what you are looking for. Perhaps the background might compete too much with your cutouts. If so, use the same colours but a different technique with the sponge. When you pick up the paints from the palette, push the sponge down several times on a clear spot on the palette. This will load the paint more evenly on the sponge. Use a quick, circular movement and skate the colour smoothly over the surface. If the paint is too heavy in any one spot, either take it off or disperse it using the other end of the sponge, which will be damp and free of paint. The main thing is not to panic.

This technique looks like glowing metal under the lacquer, and it is beautiful.

PALE CREAM OR WHITE BACKGROUND

The final colour will depend on which lacquer you apply: Estapol will give white a cream colour, Cabots' Crystal Clear will keep the background white.

Use titanium and iridescent white. Sponge on two coats of titanium white, allowing each coat to dry completely. Add a final coat of iridescent white. This gives a lustrous look and a crisp finish that reflects the light.

BLACK BACKGROUND

Do not use black alone. It is dead and not true to nature. However, if you need a black background to use as an under colour, mars black applied direct will work.

For a solid black look use two or three coats of dioxine purple. The lacquer will turn it as black as you would wish. If you do use mars black direct, add a little copper to it or glaze it over later with copper. Ultramarine blue and burnt sienna also make black. Depending on the quantities of each colour that you use, you will get either a blue-black or a brown-black.

ARABIAN NIGHT SKY BACKGROUND

Use two-thirds ultramarine blue to one-third dioxine purple. Work it wet into wet over a white background to give a beautiful background for many designs.

A MEDIAEVAL-LOOK BACKGROUND

Mix phthalocyanine blue and iridescent bronze and rub them, wet into wet, with a sponge.

FAIRY BACKGROUND

Paint the background titanium white. Allow it to dry. Soften it with iridescent white mixed separately with a microscopic amount of crimson, cobalt blue or a touch of iridescent gold here and there. If witches or goblins are to appear in your design try burnt umber, iridescent gold and copper applied wet into wet around the base of your design, shading it upwards to pure iridescent gold at the top. This gives a great atmosphere.

BACKGROUNDS FOR PHOTOGRAPHS

With age the tone of black and white photographs may vary. Sometimes they appear to have a blue look, in which case you could use a mixture of cobalt blue and iridescent bronze mixed wet into wet as your background. Others fade to a faintly green tinge. For these try a mixture of iridescent bronze and gold rubbed over a black background.

With sepia photographs, burnt umber with iridescent copper and gold worked wet into wet will give a warm, soft look. Allow it to dry and then wipe over with a fine layer of iridescent white.

The background for colour photographs will entirely depend on the subject matter of the picture. If it is a child in a garden, for example, you might like to pick up the feel of the garden. However, if it is photo of someone on their graduation day, you may feel a more formal and subdued colour is suitable.

CHRISTMAS BACKGROUNDS

If you have a Christmas theme, it is usually safe to stick to three basic shades that represent Christmas.

- Red: use equal parts of crimson and cadmium red.
- Green: use pure phthalocyanine green.
- Cream: use titanium white that has dried and been overlayed with iridescent white.

You can add a hint of sparkle with glitter or a dash of mother-of-pearl dust. Just sprinkle the powder on some polymer medium, which has been applied over the dried paint.

GLAZED OPAQUE BACKGROUND

To glaze an opaque background, follow the steps below.

1. Apply gesso. Allow it to dry well and sand it until it is completely smooth. Mix cadmium yellow on the palette, watering it down until it is a very thin consistency and delicately coloured. Use a soft sabeline brush, loaded with the paint, to drizzle the paint over the gesso, allowing the paint to run off the object. Apply three coats of the glaze, allowing each coat to dry before applying the next.

3. When the cadmium yellow glaze is dry, drizzle one or two coats of burnt umber glazes over them in the same way. You can make the paint run in any direction you wish by holding the object at a different angle.

4. Another effect can be obtained by beginning with a soft cadmium yellow and white opaque background. Allow this to dry, then apply a series of glazes in varying tones of green. Begin with the lightest shade and work to the darkest green. The finished appearance will be as if you are looking through green vines into the sunlight.

You may experiment with all of the above backgrounds but always make sure that your background harmonises with your design. Remember to keep it to the mood, style, movement and tonal value of the cutouts.

The painting must never dominate to the point where the design is overwhelmed or lost. Of course, there are exceptions to every rule and you may wish to have your design sink into the background. You may, for example, paint your background to resemble an old stone wall and have cutouts of ancient Greek stone carvings, which you wish to disappear into the background. Your whole concept might be that the viewer has to search for these designs.

The main thing is to be relaxed when you are applying the paint. If you hate the whole thing when you have finished the last stroke, and if it is still damp, wipe it off with a wet sponge. If it has dried, simply cover the whole thing with gesso and begin again. Above all, experiment and enjoy. Painting is creative and personal and is the greatest fun.

GLUING

The methods for gluing the cutouts are all quite logical. I find that four different types of glue cover all eventualities.

Each glue is used with different techniques and for different resources, so read the following information very carefully.

- Liquitex Gloss (or Matt) Medium and Varnish.
  (Atelier and Matisse also make a similar product, just make sure that whatever brand you choose mentions that it is a good adhesive.)
- Selley's Aquadhere, this is a PVA woodworking glue.
- Wallpaper paste, buy a good quality one and mix it in a jar to a thick consistency.
- A good craft glue that will glue metals.

LIQUITEX GLOSS MEDIUM AND VARNISH

This glue is the one most often used because the bulk of resources are of a weight suited to it; for example, wrapping paper, colour copying paper, good quality magazines, pages from books, etc. It is quick drying and permanent, so only glue a small section at a time and use a fine 00 sabeline brush. Begin at the widest part of your design. Remove the blu-tack in that area, but if you are fearful of losing the exact place, secure an edge of the cutout with the blu-tack on top of the design. Make certain you have removed every trace of blu-tack underneath before gluing. If you find it hard to remove, the easiest and surest way to do so is to lift it off with another piece of blu-tack. Before gluing anything, always have at least eight or nine small pieces of kitchen sponge that have been moistened and squeezed out until they are just damp.

Now lift the edge of the widest part of the design well away from the blu-tack anchoring it to the base and glue no more than 1.25 cm (½ in). Spread the glue generously on that area of the paper, push the cutout into place with the brush and then press down firmly once with a piece of damp kitchen sponge. Let this glued area dry for a couple of minutes, then remove any remaining blu-tack as this cutout is now secured. Lift the unglued section of the cutout and continue gluing, little by little. No air bubbles should be left. I have seen one rise up through 30 coats of lacquer. There is a solution to this, but it's best to avoid the problem. Above all, keep your fingers off the cutouts. If, however, you are one of those people who can't resist touching, dip your finger in the glue before touching, otherwise it could stick to the paper and remove some of the colour.

If you have glued something down by mistake and wish to remove it, you can do so, as long as it hasn't quite dried, by moistening a cotton bud with water and gently coaxing off the paper. A toothpick might also be of help. If the worst comes to the worst and you have to literally scrape it off, this will, of course, affect the paint underneath and you will have to repair it, allow it to dry and begin again. Never force your cutouts to go against their natural inclinations when easing them onto the object. If you want to change direction, cut the paper and rejoin it in the direction you want. This will avoid any creases.

Be very careful when you overlap cutouts that no air pockets are left. Press the brush firmly into the overlap area. The wooden end of your brush can also be used – roll it over an area if you suspect that all the glue has not been pressed out. Wipe off any excess glue as you go with a clean damp sponge, but there is no need to be too fussy as the glue will dry clear and not be noticeable.

AQUADHERE

This is a heavier glue used mainly for thicker cutouts, such as photographs, cards or thick calendars. It takes longer to dry and is best used in smaller quantities so that barely any is pushed out when the print is pressed into place. Apply the glue thoroughly but lightly to the back of the print, hold it in the air for a few minutes so it becomes tacky, then press the cutout into place. Clean up any excess glue from the edges and, if working on a flat surface, place something heavy such as a telephone book over it. Leave for 20 minutes or so. eg. If you have a paper that you feel is between these two thicknesses, water down the Aquadhere a little on your palette.

WALLPAPER PASTE

Wallpaper paste, mixed to a thick consistency, is best used for gluing prints over a large area; for example, the central theme of your design. The method is quite different here. Lots of glue is applied to the surface of the object and the print is laid gently into place upon it.

There are different techniques used for flat and curved surfaces.

FLAT SURFACE

After the print has been positioned carefully, press one end of it with glue-moistened fingertips and, using a rubber roller, roll from the centre of the print, pushing the glue to the edge furtherest from your fingers. Turn the object around and repeat the process on the other side. Remove your fingers as the print will now be secure and continue to push the rubber roller from the centre outwards in all directions. Use a damp sponge or a damp, lint-free cloth to remove excess glue. Again, don't be too fussy as it will dry clear, just don't leave any great lumps of glue. Wash the roller immediately, for the glue will already be drying on it. Now hold your glued section up to the light and make sure it has adhered evenly. If you suspect there is a small air bubble, dip your finger in the glue and press the cutout on that area working the bubble to the nearest edge. If you suspect a larger air bubble, use a clean rubber roller to move it to the edge (remember to wash the roller after use).

CURVED SURFACES

This requires courage and much more care for it is the most difficult part of gluing. First, when gluing on any curve, even a gentle one such as an oval soap, and whatever glue you are using, you must cut into the cutout further to allow it to stretch. I am referring to a large print on a curved surface where extensive cutting is required. This will be especially true if the curve becomes sharper at one end. Look for a line in the cutout, maybe a fold in a dress or the line of an arm or a flower petal, branch of a tree, etc. and cut along it boldly. Students often have nervous twitches when I first show them how to tackle this. Depending on the steepness of the object's curve, the print sometimes has to be cut in all directions so some parts of it are almost severed. It's a scary experience when you do it the first time, so don't be in a hurry. You have lots and lots of glue and it will remain moist enough to work with for ages. Hold your cut print in the palm of your hand and gently place it in position on the glued surface. If you are worried that you will forget where you positioned it, leave a rolled up piece of blu-tack about 2.5 cm (1 in) above where the top of your print is to be. With plenty of glue on your fingers (you don't want any faceless cherubs or arms missing from your print) gently tap the pieces into position, overlapping them where necessary (and there will be overlaps caused by the shape of the object on which you are working). Concentrate hard at this point. Do not tuck under parts that should be on top; for example, folds in a dress, feet, chimneys, baskets resting on something, lake edges – the possibilities are endless! If you have pressed the wrong section on top, gently lift it and reposition the pieces.

At this stage, you are still working with masses of moist glue, so changes are no problem. Do not be alarmed if you find an area where the edges don't quite meet and, because of the shape, you cannot bridge the gap. It simply means that background colour will show through in a narrow area in the middle of your print. It can be easily painted later in the appropriate colours and will not be seen once there are layers of lacquer over the top. Naturally, try not to have this problem occurring in the middle of something complicated like a face!

Once the print is in position, very gently roll out the excess glue with the rubber roller towards the nearest edges. You will have many edges because of the extensive cutting of the print and this is an advantage as you don't have to move the glue very far. If it looks good, wipe off the excess glue and begin to roll more firmly to get the last of the excess glue out. Clean the glue off and hold the piece up to a good light so that you can differentiate between the bumps of overlapping cutouts (and perhaps a fine gap or two) and air pockets or pockets of excess glue. Do not worry about the small bumps caused by excess glue, they can be left to join the other uneven areas in the print and none will be visible by the time you have completed the lacquering (but do take care of any air pockets).

CRAFT GLUE FOR METALS

This glue is used for sticking any metallic papers or for attaching brass ribbon holders to hanging eggs or Christmas decorations. Other uses are for gluing back a layer of lacquer that you have cut open to release air or rescue a forgotten piece of blu-tack beneath the lacquer, repairing a crack in your object before you commence work, or a break when you drop it while working on it.

These glues take longer to dry and some of them generate 'spider threads'. Ignore these, just clean them off when you have finished. Even if they are dry, they break off quite easily. Once the glue has been pressed out, clean up and then do not touch anything for at least two days (depending on the weather). If any strain is to be placed on this glue; for example, a large hanging ball, leave it for a week to dry.

Apply this glue to both surfaces, allow a few minutes for it to become tacky, then press the surfaces together with a minimum of fuss, it dries clear and is best handled as little as possible.

AIR BUBBLES

If you spot these at the time of gluing, they are easily remedied by pushing glue underneath the cutout to that area or by adding more glue with a fine brush in that area and re-pressing the cutout down firmly. However, if the air bubble is not noticed until you are partially through or have completed the lacquering process, it can still be fixed. Take courage and cut right down to and through the print with a stanley knife, trying to follow a line of the design. Lift the cut edge, insert some craft glue with a 00 brush and press firmly with a sponge. Clean up any excess glue on the lacquer, then press firmly again with a fresh, damp sponge and hold in place for 10 minutes or so. Leave it overnight to dry, then sand gently any lumps you have caused and repair any other damage with paint and resume lacquering. Once you have finished, you'll never see it. If you have overlooked creases in your gluing, you will probably find them when you sand, as their level will be higher than the rest of the surface and it is likely that you will sand it back so that the cutout is white before you know it. Don't worry! Just repair the damage with a little matching, watered-down paint and re-seal the area with polymer medium before your next coat of lacquer.

Gluing is very straight forward. Just remember the following points.
- Select the right glue for your cutout.
- Glue from wide to narrow.
- Always cut the design to make it go the direction you want.
- Avoid air bubbles. (If you suspect one when lacquering, test by rubbing your finger across it and you will see it move. If you are still not sure, hold the object up to your ear and rub your thumb firmly over the suspected area and you can often hear a crackle; this is the noise made by the air being moved under the lacquer. Slice and repair as instructed.)
- Above all, keep your work clean and try to keep your fingers off it.

A final tip. Once you have used a piece of sponge for pressing down glued areas three times, toss it in your jar of water. When all your sponges are in the jar, rinse them thoroughly under the tap, wring out and start again. The reason for this is that glue will have begun drying on the sponge surface and this could lift up all or part of your design, so keep the sponges very clean indeed.

Gluing is an art and I just hope I have given you enough information to enable you to master that art.

SEALING CUTOUTS

All of the cut design that has been glued down must be thoroughly sealed at least twice. Not even the smallest area should remain exposed. Use a polymer medium such as the water-based glue, Liquitex Gloss Medium and Varnish, to seal the surface. Because it is water-based, it does not harm the prints. Indeed, the reverse, for it protects the prints from the lacquer, which is oil-based and can cause the prints to 'weep'.

Apply the sealant with a soft brush and leave one hour drying time between each coat. It is not necessary to seal the painted background, but I usually do even if it is not near the cutouts. I tend to seal everything, as sealing the whole object keeps the level of the surface even.

If you do not seal thoroughly, your cutouts may turn a grubby brown colour that resembles rising damp and you will either have to hand paint the original colour back meticulously or begin all over again.

Do not despair if the only area that has wept in your design is a face and you just know you can't repair it adequately with paint. Simply cut out another face and glue it on top of the damaged one. Once it is lacquered, you will never detect it.

Take great care with sealing and leave it for 24 hours after the last coat before beginning to lacquer.

SEALING PAPER BEFORE CUTTING

There are some papers, like fine rice papers, that should be sealed both sides before they are cut. A few wrapping papers require sealing also, as they are so thin or of such poor quality that gluing will cause them to weep and become blotchy. If you are in doubt about the quality and porosity of the paper that you are about to use, test a small area first to see if it weeps when glue is applied. Some papers weep slightly during gluing but dry clear. Remember this when you are testing the paper.

You may wonder why I do not simply say to seal everything first and be done with it. The reason is this: it is not so easy to cut something very finely if it has been sealed and sometimes the sealing layer comes away from the print during cutting. It's just that bit harder to cut a tiny circle when the paper is already sealed, and also a little harder to glue. Therefore, don't seal unless absolutely necessary.

Certainly newspaper must be sealed. It will weep quite dreadfully. If you are preserving a special newspaper clipping as part of your découpage, follow the instructions below.

1. Use a can of good spray fixative.

2. Lay the paper to be sealed on a much larger sheet of newspaper or butcher's paper.

3. Begin spraying well to the left of your design paper so that by the time the spray passes over it, you have a good even pressure and won't leave pools of extra sealant within the area to be used. Stop spraying only after the can has passed well to the right of the paper.

4. Leave to dry for one hour.

5. Turn the paper over and repeat the process on the other side of the print.

This method can be used on any paper you are sealing.

LACQUERING

Shellac was the lacquer traditionally used by the Venetian découpeurs, and it was sanded back with varying grades of pumice. Both materials are still used today and I find this puzzling for there are problems associated with these methods, in particular the cracking and crazing of the lacquer that occurs with time.

During my recent tour of the lacquering studios in Venice, I talked at length with the master lacquerers. Despite their admiration of, and indeed amazement, with the finish on the pieces of découpage I had taken as gifts, the light disappeared from their eyes when I informed them that it was a polyurethane lacquer and I used modern abrasives. One has to suppress feelings of frustration and simply accept the fact that their time-honoured traditions will remain unchanged and these wonderfully creative artisans are locked as firmly into the techniques of the Renaissance as they are into their traditional family structures. To accept cultural differences complete-ly is never easy, but I cannot stifle the feelings of regret when I compare the different surface finishes. A few months ago, one of the men from the Venetian Institute came to Australia. He brought me a gift – a faux-mar-bled gypsum egg finished with shellac. It was presented with great ceremony, respect and affection and I was honoured to be given it. Resolutely, I firmly pushed away any comparison between shellac and modern lacquer.

I know there are many polyurethene lacquers on the market but I can only write with any authority on two: Wattyl Estapol and Cabot's Crystal Clear. However, I have also recently been experimenting with boat lacquer for the final coats.

EQUIPMENT

Before you begin lacquering, you will need the following:

- soft 2.5 cm (1 in) synthetic (nylon or sabeline) brush
- tack cloth.
- jar of turpentine (or water if using Cabot's Crystal Clear).
- small hammer for re-sealing lid of lacquer tin.
- lever for opening lid.
- tissues.
- blu-tack.
- a well-ventilated room (wear a painter's mask if you experience any discomfort to your eyes or nose).

WATTYL ESTAPOL

I was most fortunate in the early days of experimentation to interest the inventor of Wattyl Estapol, Richard Bell, in découpage. He thought it beautiful and was amazed at the stress I was putting his product under with the number of coats being used and the continual sanding. It became a learning process for both of us.

Estapol is a very suitable lacquer for Australian climatic conditions. It has an elasticity that prevents cracking when temperatures plunge from 40 degrees to 18 degrees within an hour, as they do in some parts of the country. It also has a yellow tint that enhances most découpage background colours and causes the work to appear to glow from within.

Estapol lacquer comes in gloss, satin and matt finishes, but it is the gloss that is best for building up the coats of lacquer for découpage because the fat content is much, much higher than with the satin or matt finishes, so fewer coats are needed. Satin can be used as a final coat, however, as it containes a flow promoter and you can get a better finish with fewer brush marks. Satin and matt lacquers need to be thoroughly stirred, but do not stir the gloss.

APPLICATION

Estapol can be applied quite thickly, as long as enough curing time is left between coats. There is a world of difference between touch dry and cured. If the coat is thin, allow 24 hours drying time; if it is thick, allow two to three days.

Before you begin lacquering, check that you have thoroughly sealed off your work with Gloss Medium and Varnish. Remember that confidence is the secret. Work out your brush route and then be quick and sure.

1. Open lid of Estapol tin.

2. Rub the tack rag firmly over all the surface of the object to remove dust. (Do not expect the tack rag to remove sanding dust, just invisible dust.)

3. Dip the brush into the lacquer and go straight to the object. Do not splay the bristles on edge of tin as you will put air into the lacquer and create bubbles.

4. Apply the lacquer with the flat side of the brush, not the end. Do not splay the bristles or brush as you would house paint. Hold the brush sideways and use a light, quick motion. This must be done with a soft brush. Use plenty of lacquer.

5. When you have finished, put your brush in the jar of turpentine, suspending it on the inside top edge with the blu-tack so that the bristles do not come into contact with the bottom of the jar. When removing the brush from turpentine for next application of lacquer, hold the brush han-

dle and squeeze the bristles firmly, just once, between two thicknesses of tissue to remove the excess turpentine.

6. Place the tack rag in a screw top jar and close the lid so that it is airtight and the rag retains its tackiness.

7. Put the lid back on the tin and tap it down with a hammer. Some people invert the tin to prevent the air at the top causing a skin on the lacquer, but I can't be bothered with this as, whatever one does, once opened lacquer has a limited lifespan (usually three to four months when being used continuously).

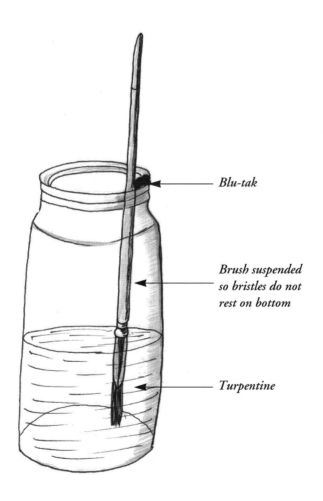

Blu-tak

Brush suspended
so bristles do not
rest on bottom

Turpentine

CABOT'S CRYSTAL CLEAR

This is a water-based lacquer so the brush is cleaned in water. It is a much thinner product and so takes many more coats to build up the necessary thickness. It is quite safe to apply two coats in a day, but this still doesn't really equal the thickness of a single coat of Estapol.

I personally only use it when I want to keep the background colour unchanged; for example, when I am using a colour such as pearl white, pale pink or blue and especially, lavender. I am too enchanted by the richness brought to my work with Estapol and too impatient with the slower build-up of lacquer to use it often. Also, I cannot recommend it with the same confidence as Estapol for it is a relatively new product and I do not know how it will look in 20 years time. However, of the water-based lacquers currently on the market, Cabot's sands quite crisply providing you allow it to cure thoroughly. An advantage is that you rarely get water marks when sanding it (see Sanding, page 54). It gives a perfectly clear finish with only the merest hint of yellowing over many coats. It dries best in warm conditions.

BOAT LACQUER

I have recently been experimenting with a boat lacquer for the four final coats. The one I have found to be compatible with Estapol is Epiglass Goldspar, although any good brand of boat lacquer would suffice. This dries to a very hard finish and although wet-and-dry sanding with No. 1200 paper may produce a faint water-mark, it is easily removed with the micro-mesh. It also has a high level of UV inhibitors, which should help protect the prints. The surface flexibility is good so it guards against chipping.

I apply four final coats after the final sanding of the Estapol with No. 320 sandpaper and leave the lacquer to cure for four weeks before sanding with No. 1200 wet-and-dry sandpaper. This lacquer takes longer to become touch-dry than Estapol or Cabot's.

METHOD

Each object will present its own problems, there is no single rule for lacquering techniques.

EGGS

Eggs can be difficult to work, but you can dip them in the lacquer by securing a wooden shashlik stick through the bottom hole. Immerse the egg in the lacquer, then hold it above the tin and allow the excess lacquer to run off. However, the very second that the run of lacquer develops into a drip, twist the stick around, invert the egg and stand the stick upright in a container so that the lacquer can run down the egg to the stick in the opposite direction. If you delay during this procedure and wait until there are several drips, the lacquer will already have begun to dry slightly and it will not run easily in the opposite direction down to the stick. It will resist the change of direction and be sluggish, not reaching the stick but forming a drip.

Do not use old lacquer on eggs as it flows too slowly.

The stand I use when lacquering eggs is an old block of wood into which I've drilled small holes. I then stand this wood on aluminium foil, because there is a mess as the lacquer runs off the egg and down the stick. If you are a frugal person you must steel yourself to some lacquer wastage with this process! A word of warning. Do not stand your stick in styrene or florist's foam, for the lacquer will gobble it up (or, to be less dramatic, dissolve it.) The egg must remain perfectly upright, so the stick must be secure. A jar filled with sand or rice works well also, but you will find your own ingenious method.

Never handle your object while lacquering it. Secure it to another object and handle that. For instance, blu-tack a box lid or base to the top of a sturdy jar and turn the jar rather than the box. A turntable is essential for cylinders. If you can't procure one, use an old plate, which can be turned as you work – this will not be as quick, however.

FLAT SURFACES

To lacquer a flat surface, such as the panel of a screen, a plaque or a box, concentrate on applying the lacquer around the edges of the flat surface. It is then easy to fill in the centre without the lacquer spilling over the edges. Ten minutes or so after lacquering, return and make sure it has not crept over the edge. If it has, remove the drips with turpentine (if using Estapol) or water (if using Cabot's) with a moistened tissue.

Lacquer only on the horizontal surfaces of an object. If you have lacquered the top of a box, leave it for a few hours, then turn it over and do the sides one by one. In the long run this is much quicker and you will avoid drips.

When lacquering a tray, avoid a build up of lacquer at the edges and corners. Lacquer thinly in these areas for they are hard to sand later if the lacquer is too thick. The perfect solution is to work on a tray where the base and sides have been left separate by the carpenter.

UPRIGHT CYLINDRICAL SHAPES

To lacquer an upright vase, urn or pot, whether it is round, hexagonal or square, it is most helpful to have a turntable – a 'lazy Susan' is ideal. Find the lid of a jar which is smaller than the base of your object and firmly blu-tack it to the middle of your turntable. Then secure the object to the lid the same way. This allows the lacquer to run off the base of the object without sticking and facilitates rapid lacquering, which always produces the best results. Begin at the top and apply lacquer around the object working down to the base. Lightly (like the touch of a butterfly) and quickly move the brush upwards then downwards, and leave it alone.

At the end of lacquering, you will have a messy, unfinished base. Before your final sanding, remove the mess and paint the base. Allow it to dry thoroughly before applying three or four coats of lacquer.

You may like to sign and date your work at this stage. A pen with permanent ink can be used for this or a fine brush with paint mixed to a flowing consistency. I often use the following method. First paint the base with a dark or light colour. Allow it to dry thoroughly. Apply a thick, contrasting coat over the base and, while it is still wet, use the pointed end of a shashlik stick to write your name and date. The top coat of paint is removed as you do this, leaving the contrasting colour below showing through. Apply the final coats of lacquer.

Signing through wet paint

HOW MANY COATS OF LACQUER ARE NEEDED?

This is the question most often asked. There is no definite answer to it because it depends on several factors.

- How thick each coat of the lacquer is.
- How much background lacquer is being sanded off as you go.
- How thick the cutouts are.
- Whether there are overlapping cutouts, which raises their level in certain areas.

Here are some rough guidelines which may be of help, but do take the above factors into account.

- Eggs: seven or eight dips.
- Flat surfaces: 12 to 14 coats.
- Upright cylindrical shapes: anywhere between 15 and 25 coats.

I am reluctant to give even these rough figures, for lacquering is very individual. As you become more skilled, you will develop an instinct as to when there are enough coats on to sand safely but, until you do, you might like to keep a tally of the coats you are applying. Do not begin to sand until at least five coats have been applied and read the chapter on sanding carefully.

HELPFUL HINTS

1. Drips are not a real worry, they can be sanded off.

2. Look carefully for hairs along the way and remove them with the sharp end of a razor blade. A hair embedded deep in the lacquer – perhaps as far back as the gluing stage – cannot be retrieved and is best disguised with a touch of paint.

3. Don't splay the bristles of the brush on the side of the tin or on your work. Apply lacquer with the flat side of the brush, holding it almost horizontal.

4. Lacquer quickly and surely; try not to go over and over because the lacquer begins drying immediately and will drag the brush, leaving uneven marks.

5. Suspend the brush in turpentine or water (depending on whether you are using Estapol or Cabot's) between applications.

6. If using Estapol, change the turpentine weekly as a chemical reaction occurs between the turpentine and lacquer, which results in a gelatinous substance forming. Once this gets into the bristles, it is hard to eradicate. If it does, leave the brush in nail-varnish remover for three minutes. Rinse in clean turpentine twice, lather with soap and warm water and rinse very thoroughly to make sure all traces of soap are removed. Finally, rinse it in cold water, squeeze the excess water out with your fingers, gently press bristles back into shape and leave in a jar to dry with the bristles pointing upwards.

   If you don't plan to lacquer for a few weeks, remove the brush from the turpentine and rinse thoroughly in two lots of clean turpentine. Massage the bristles with warm water and laundry soap, rinsing out the latter meticulously and ending with a cold water rinse. Re-shape the bristles and leave upright to dry.

7. If using Cabot's Crystal Clear, wash the brush in warm, soapy water, then rinse thoroughly to remove all traces of soap. Finally, rinse in cold water, squeeze the excess water out with your fingers, press the bristles

back into shape and leave to dry in a jar with the bristles pointing upwards.

8. Don't worry too much about dust: it is inevitable. Oriental lacquering is often done at sea to avoid it. If you ever observe a sunbeam in your house, you will see particles of dust spinning around it. I take only two reasonable precautions.

- Don't lacquer in the same room where you have been sanding.
- Do not wear woollen garments, unless they are covered by a smock, when lacquering as fine hairs from the fibre will become attached to the wet lacquer.

9. When the lacquer tin is opened and ready, remove brush from the turpentine or water without splaying the bristles against the rim. Remove any excess liquid by one firm squeeze of the bristles between tissues.

10. Always secure your object to something that you can handle. If you are working on a small lid, secure it underneath with blu-tack to a tomato sauce bottle, then hold the bottle as you work. If very heavy drips form at the base of your object, they can either be removed during, or at the end of the lacquering process with a stanley knife, then sanded smooth. Great care should be taken when slicing a drip to only remove the main part of it, and then sandpaper it to the level of the surrounding surface.

11. Keep the object level so that the lacquer does not gravitate to one side.

12. Avoid lacquering on a day of high humidity. It can affect the flow and make drying more difficult. A good windy day is ideal as the lacquer requires aeration for drying, not heat.

13. Before applying each coat of lacquer, wipe over the object with a tack cloth. Dust and hairs do sand off, but this precaution keeps them to a minimum.

14. The final coats should by applied as thickly and evenly as possible and left to cure for three to four weeks before final finishing begins. If you have trouble applying an even coat of gloss at this stage, try using Satin Estapol. It has a flow promoter in it and the lacquer runs more easily.

15. If a skin has formed over the lacquer in the tin, break it to reach the lacquer underneath. This lacquer is now old, thicker and more yellow, but can still be used safely on dark backgrounds. Do not use it for light backgrounds as it will quickly turn pale blue to green, creams to yellow, pale pinks to apricot, and so on. Open a fresh tin for lighter backgrounds.

16. A lacquered object must never be left in direct sunlight, particularly in a car. The temperature in a car, even on a cloudy day, can be high. This makes the lacquer soften and expand into a bubble. Should this happen to you, leave the whole thing in a cool environment for three weeks and it will subside. You may then just need to do a little re-lacquering and sanding. Putting it too close to a fire can also result in this damage.

17. Lacquer takes a good 12 months to cure thoroughly, so don't subject placemats or tables to use in that time; just enjoy looking at them!

18. You may be tempted to slice off an extra large drip that hasn't hardened, but this can cause trouble. If a drip feels soft, leave it alone and allow it to harden further. Attempting this while it is still soft may damage the surrounding lacquer also. The sticky lacquer in the drip may catch in the sandpaper and cause the surrounding lacquer to be pulled away from the surface.

19. If your lacquer becomes crazed or wrinkled during drying, it is because the last coat was applied over a coat that has not cured properly. It may have been dry to touch, but was not hard and, therefore, was technically still drying. The last coat, which was also trying to dry, was being distorted by the coat underneath. Do not panic. Just leave the whole thing for a week, then sand off the wrinkles. The same problem may occur if lacquer is applied over a moist surface (perhaps some water has been left when cleaning off sanding dust). Always keep your work dry.

To test how hard the lacquer is, press the tip of your nail into the surface and it shouldn't cause too much of a dent.

20. If, inexplicably, your last coat of lacquer begins peeling off when dry, this may be because your object has been left standing for a few weeks

between coats of lacquer. To avoid this, a light sand must be given to the surface to allow the fresh coat to bond to the previous one. If peeling does occur, every bit of lacquer must be peeled off – rather like skin which has been sunburnt. Use your nail, or a soft, blunt instrument like a cuticle orange stick. Once it has all been removed, sand thoroughly and re-lacquer.

Lacquer may also peel off if it is applied straight on existing polished wood. Two coats of polymer medium should be applied over the surface before lacquering. The same applies to natural wood or wood that has been oiled. You must protect the surface from the lacquer, as some lacquers do not agree chemically with oiled surfaces.

21. Lacquer may sometimes swell. With horror, you observe a partially finished piece develop a large, raised bump that feels loose to touch. This happens mainly with egg shells, bisque or terracotta, all of which are highly porous. The bump means that moisture has seeped in from behind your work, either through a tiny crack in the inner glaze or straight through the egg shell or unsealed terracotta. The moisture has lifted your design, paint and lacquer into a bump. The moisture usually comes from the wet-and-dry sanding or micromesh process, but perspiration can also be the cause if you have held, for example, a tall vase by inserting your hand and arm into it while working. All is not lost! Let it dry out for two to three weeks and it will diminish, sometimes disappearing altogether. If the bump doesn't disappear, surgery is required. Be brave. Use a stanley knife and lance the bubble four ways. Peel it back slightly and glue the four sections back in place with wood glue. You may have a bit of overlapping, but this is not a problem. Leave the glue to set for two days, sand the overlapping area until it is smooth, retouch the colour with paint and re-apply the lacquer. No one will ever know it was there. To avoid this problem, take great care to push a towel inside a large object to absorb moisture and when working with eggs, seal off the hole with your thumb when using water. Leave the egg a week before sealing the hole. Always hold the egg so that the hole is at the bottom as you work and use the least amount of water possible.

SANDING

Of all the technical stages of découpage, sanding is probably the most important. Poor lacquering can be rescued with sanding, while lumps, bumps, grit, moth wings, brush marks, hairs and dust can be magically removed. Sanding provides the base to enable the next coat to bond.

During my early years of découpage, I experimented with many grits and brands of sandpaper. What became very clear to me that it is vital to have a good sanding block. It is not possible to sand evenly holding the sandpaper with your fingers as it is impossible to keep an even pressure over a large area. For wet-and-dry sandpaper, I use a firm foam block and for silicon carbide stearate papers, I use a Swiss manufactured block that is spongy on one side and hard on the other. Both sides of the Swiss block have a velcro surface so that the German sandpapers can be adhered to it.

A block ensures that sanding is even, which is vital, while the spongy side keeps the work air-cooled so that there is no heat build-up. You hold it very lightly and the sandpaper does all the work for you. In fact, the less pressure you apply, the quicker you will be.

Sanding with wet-and-dry sandpapers is a slow and laborious process that risks water damage to the work. I wanted something that would sand much faster, leave fewer scratches and have its own built-in lubricant. The German stearate sandpapers are ideal and cut the lacquer crisply and quickly.

This leads me to emphasise the need, during the initial stages of sanding, to keep taking the lacquer off the print, not off the background. Students often have great trouble in accepting that on a completed piece of découpage, no matter how many coats you have had to apply, there should only be two or three coats of lacquer on the cutouts. If there are more than this, you have a buried print and you may just as well have put a sheet of glass over the whole thing in the first place. On the background you may have between 10 and 30 coats, but not on the cutouts. Your cutouts and prints must be as level with your background as possible so that the whole surface looks handpainted. With a good piece it is hard to identify if it is découpage or handpainted, even with a magnifying glass.

The Melbourne National Gallery has some fine eighteenth-century pieces of découpage that are listed as handpainted.

A good test for your work is to look at the print and see if it has changed colour. It should not have, for it is barely covered with lacquer, whereas the background colour may have changed considerably.

When you reach the final stages of sanding and have sanded back to the print, perhaps even removing a scrap of it, then this is good sanding. Repair any damage by touching up the tiny bit of print you have removed with a 00 brush and watered-down paint, and continue to lacquer.

EQUIPMENT

I use the following equipment for all stages of sanding of the lacquer, including the finishing process.

- No. 320 German Siafast silicon carbide stearate sandpaper. This has a velcro surface and is sized to fit the block. You should also have a plain-backed sheet of the same paper.
- No. 280 German Siafast silicon carbide stearate sandpaper with a velcro surface, for working on water-based lacquers.
- No. 1200 wet-and-dry sandpaper.
- No. 4000 micro-mesh, used with a foam block.
- No. 6000 micro-mesh, used with a foam block.
- No. 8000 micro-mesh, used with a foam block.
- No. 12000 micro-mesh, used with a foam block.
- Swiss Siafast sanding block.
- Lint-free cloth (such as a chamois).
- Towel.
- No. 120 silicon carbide stearate sandpaper. This is used with the Swiss block and is a coarser paper, suitable for preparing wood and sanding gesso, which dries very hard and needs a stronger paper.

METHOD

When you are ready to sand your work, sit comfortably with a towel across your knees. Use one side of the towel to wipe any dust off the object and the other side for wiping the block clear of dust. Both these actions are important. If you looked at sandpaper under an electron microscope you would see its teeth.

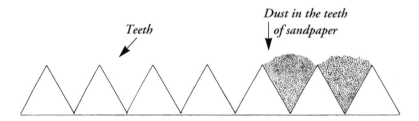

Dust builds up into the teeth, spilling over and making little white dots on the paper. This means the sandpaper is no longer efficient and the clogs of dust will scratch the lacquer. So keep both the sandpaper and surface clean with the towel.

If sanding for any length of time, try to sit outdoors so the dust doesn't irritate your nose and eyes. If I'm sanding something large, I wear a mask, goggles and smock.

After each sanding is finished, wipe the work with a damp, lint-free cloth. Do not use your tack rag to do this: its function is to remove invisible dust just before lacquering.

Begin sanding after you have applied between five and seven coats. Use the No. 320 sandpaper fastened to the block. Hold it gently and sand very lightly, just enough to remove surface dust and to give a key for subsequent coats of lacquer. It doesn't matter with this grit whether you sand up or down or around and around – most people tend to the latter – just do not apply pressure.

From now on, sand in this way every third or so coat of lacquer, but concentrate on taking lacquer off the cutouts and just tidying the lacquer on the background. Naturally, this tidying of the background lacquer means removing drips, runs and serious brush marks. If a drip feels soft, cease sanding and wait a few days for it to cure and harden.

Sometimes you come across a little circle of lacquer that defies sanding. A white rim around the circle persistently remains. This has been caused by a drip of lacquer falling from the brush that has not been thoroughly sanded back along the way. It leaves a little air hollow. If you can't remove the white edges, as a last resort, just paint over them and continue lacquering. If the trouble spot is on a cutout, it is safer to pursue this course rather than risk sanding back to the paper.

On average, depending on the thickness of the cutouts, once you have applied between 15 and 20 coats of lacquer, you should be ready for the final major sand. It is at this stage you are levelling the cutout images with the background.

Using the block and No. 320 stearate sandpaper, sand evenly in a circular motion until the entire surface presents a dull, matt appearance. With Estapol, you will notice water-wave markings (a bit like moiré silk taffeta) at this time, which have a dull sheen but feel as smooth as silk. This is normal. I think they occur where one layer of lacquer has met the next unevenly. These water-wave markings must not be confused with shiny spots or lines of shine, which must still be removed. These spots or lines are levels that dip into the lacquer below your finished surface. If you rub the tips of your fingers lightly over them, you should feel a slight bump. Lack of sensitivity in your fingertips may not allow you to feel them, in which case, hold your work up to the light and trust to your vision. What they actually look like, magnified and from the side, is shown below.

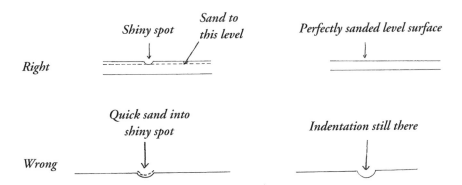

A trap to be aware of sometimes occurs when the major sand looks right – no shiny spots, just water-waves on a dull surface – but, the cutout still feels slightly undulating to the touch. If you do not sand back further on these areas and remove the excess lacquer from them, the final finish will only highlight the undulations and you will be disappointed. At this stage, the whole surface area must be completely even with only two or three coats of lacquer left on the cutouts.

You must be really tough at this point. The final finish will never be perfect if the major sand is not done properly.

Once it is perfectly smooth, apply two final, thick coats if you are using Estapol, or four light, but covering, coats if you are using boat lacquer or Cabot's Crystal Clear. This time it is important to have as little dust as possible on the surface and certainly no drips, runs or brush marks. Now set your work aside for two to three weeks in a place with a good air-flow for the final coats to cure and harden.

I know it is hard to wait for the curing, but it is vital that the lacquer be hard before the final finishing stages. Both boat lacquer and Cabot's Crystal Clear take much longer to harden than Estapol. In fact, if using the Cabot's throughout, the longer you leave it to cure between each and every application, the better it will be during sanding. At the major sanding stage with Cabot's, use the heavier No. 280 sandpaper, but finish with the No. 320 to remove any excess scratching before the final coats of lacquer are applied.

HELPFUL HINTS

1. If you find you have a well-buried hair, on no account sand right back to get at the hair. However, first do have a good sand to make sure it really is buried if you are unable to ascertain it visually. If the hair is deeply embedded, repair it as follows. Apply lacquer lightly and allow it to dry. Match some paint to the colour surrounding the hair and mix it to the consistency of milk. Using the very tip of a 00 brush, make tiny dots of paint over the hair – like the dots in a newspaper photograph. When the paint is dry, continue lacquering.

2. Never make paint repairs immediately after your work has been sanded, as it is impossible to match the colours exactly. Apply a light coat of lacquer first so that you can match the colour accurately. Always make any paint repairs on a lacquered surface, not a sanded one. Never make repairs using any of the iridescent shades, as they seem to jump out on top of the lacquer.

3. For those areas that cannot be reached by the sandpaper on a block use a plain sheet of No. 320 sandpaper, which has been cut to fit. For instance, to reach into the corner of a tray, just tear off a section of the No. 320 sandpaper and fold it once or twice. The sandpaper can even be folded to form a sharp point to reach right into the corner.

4. Allergy sufferers should use a good quality wet-and-dry No. 320 sandpaper wrapped around a foam block (such as the one that comes with the micro-mesh kit). It won't be as fast or as efficient but it does not leave any dust to float and irritate your nose. Remember to be careful to clean off the messy residue thoroughly. If you leave any on, a bloom will occur under subsequent coats of lacquer. Take care with the water, particularly if working with something porous, so that it doesn't damage your object.

FINISHING

The last coats of lacquer have cured and hardened and it is time to remove the dust and begin the final finish. I have listed the equipment you will need for this stage on page 43.

PREPARATION

Use a foam block (there is one in the micro-mesh kit if you have one, otherwise any off-cut of firm foam will suffice) and wrap a piece of No. 1200 wet-and-dry sandpaper around it. Just cut the No. 1200 sandpaper to fit your block. Moisten both the block and sandpaper; either place them under a running tap or have a bowl of water beside you. If you suspect you are a bit heavy-handed, use soapy water to help the sandpaper glide over the surface.

Sand back and forth in one direction only. Work very lightly. Don't scrub, just glide the wet-and-dry sandpaper gently over the surface until all dust marks have gone and the surface is matt, with only the finest of scratch marks.

Finally, hold your object up to the light and if you see too many scratch marks, rub gently in the other direction.

You must not sand so hard that you reach the point where the final coat of lacquer joins the previous coat. If you are sanding really gently you won't. If you do, you will get a water-wave effect that is hard to eradicate. If this does happen, apply another final coat of lacquer, allow it to cure and then sand gently. Epiglass boat lacquer does produce a faint water-wave mark but this will disappear as you sand with micro-mesh. Cabot's Crystal Clear leaves no water-wave marks.

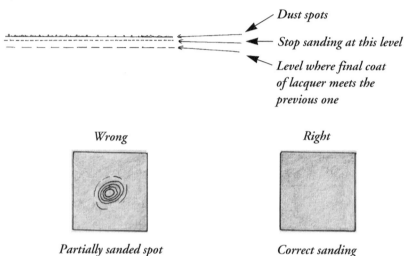

Dust spots

Stop sanding at this level

Level where final coat of lacquer meets the previous one

Wrong

Right

Partially sanded spot

Correct sanding

Wipe all residue of soapy water thoroughly from your work. Any soap left on will cause a film and mar the finished glow.

Be sure to note the direction you sanded last with the No.1200 wet-and-dry sandpaper before beginning the micro-mesh process. It is vital to work in a different direction with each of the different grit sandpapers during the next stage.

MICRO-MESH FINISH

Clear instructions will come as part of your micro-mesh kit, but I would just like to add some more detail.

1. Wrap No. 4000 sandpaper around the foam block and, using water, begin rubbing in the opposite direction to the way you sanded with the No. 1200 wet-and-dry sandpaper. Do not exert pressure. Take an area of about 15 cm (6 in) square and work back and forth for about 50 seconds. Remember the direction you have been sanding.

2. Wipe the surface of the object dry with a towel. Rinse the No. 4000 sandpaper under running water (there will be a residue on it although you will not be able to see it), lay it flat and leave to dry.

3. Using No. 6000 sandpaper, cross hatch sand in the opposite direction. Repeat the cleaning steps as for 2 above. You will note that there is now a magically silky surface with a low sheen. If you like it and it suits your piece, you can stop.

4. For a deeper glow, continue sanding in different directions with the No. 8000 and No. 12000 sandpapers.

5. If you wish to have an even higher gloss finish, a little liquid car wax applied quickly and polished with a soft rag will bring up the sheen to a very high gloss.

6. Always keep the micro-mesh (wet or dry) in the calico bag provided. This allows it to breathe and keeps dust and light from damaging it.

What the micro-mesh is doing is cutting and polishing the lacquer so that it loses the slightest look of polyurethane and resembles the finest porcelain.

The greatest advantage of this finishing method is that it is quick, fingers will not mark it and, in a 100 years' time, it will still have the same glow. If it has sat upon Aunt Ada's shelf for 50 years and become covered in dust and grime, a wash with warm, soapy water will bring it back to new. A kit will cover the area of a Rolls Royce motor car, so it will last through many pieces of découpage.

Waxes and polishes of any sort do not last for ever and must be re-done from time to time to keep the découpage fresh. I feel I may not be able to rely on my descendants for this constant care, so was overjoyed to discover micro-mesh, which gives découpage that lovely tactile quality so easily.

OTHER FINISHES

If you don't have a micro-mesh kit available to you, experiment with the following.

- A good furniture wax.

- A water-based rubbing compound, followed by a good quality car wax.
- 000 steel wool dipped into a commercial finishing compound. Wet steel wool will provide a more abrasive action if you are trying to get rid of some No. 1200 wet-and-dry sandpaper scratch marks.

In all instances, use a soft cloth with waxes, and polish in one direction only, working on a very small area at any one time. Waxes are applied after the final sanding with No. 1200 wet-and-dry sandpaper.

Over the years, I have experimented with everything from beeswax to the latest car polish and while some have achieved a satisfactory result, they are not to be compared with the micro-mesh finish. I find it hard to be enthusiastic about other finishes, but if you discover one you love, stick to it for, after all, it is only you who is the judge.

DÉCOUPAGE UNDER GLASS

During the nineteenth century, it was fashionable to simulate ancient Chinese porcelain by adhering coloured cutouts to the back of glass. This process was originally known as 'potichomania'. Very beautiful effects can be achieved, but you need to have a lot of patience for the gluing is very fiddly and takes time. The technique is the complete opposite to other types of gluing. This time you are not pressing all the glue out and the glue is placed on the front of the cutout, which is then pressed on the underside of the glass.

EQUIPMENT

You will need the following items:
- a clear glass object (a plate or flat piece of glass is best to begin with)
- cutout design
- PVA wood glue, such as Selleys
- cotton buds
- tissues
- lint-free cloth
- water
- vinegar

- polymer medium for sealant
- pieces of kitchen sponge dampened
- paints
- gesso
- toothpicks
- lacquer

CUTOUTS

If this is your first attempt, I strongly recommend that you only use one simple shape – perhaps an apple, a pear or a round shape depicting something that appeals to you.

Most important, the weight of the paper must be right. Anything cut from a book or calendar is ideal. It is not as thick as card, but not as flimsy as wrapping paper. As you become more skilled, you can try other weights, but the gluing is more difficult.

GLASS OBJECTS

Hunt through gift shops for glass plates. The only requirement is that the glass is clear and that the manufacturer's name does not appear on it, for this is very hard to disguise. Years ago, some fine Swedish and French plates were readily available in Melbourne. These appear to have disappeared from the market place, but it is still possible to locate round and oval plates.

Other glass objects that you can use are as follows:
- Old hurricane lamps (as long as you can fit your hand inside)
- The sort of glass jar with a lid that is often used for cotton balls or buds.
- Glass bowl, or vase with a wide neck.
- Glass suppliers will cut glass to any shape, so you may wish to work on a glass oval that can be framed, or cover a small coffee table or desk top.

PREPARATION

The first task is to wash the glass in warm soapy water. Using a mixture of white vinegar and water, thoroughly clean the back of the plate, then dry it with a lint-free cloth. This will remove any grease spots or residue of soap and leave it squeaky clean. From now on, hold it with the palms of your hands pressed against the edges, otherwise you will leave grease from your fingers on the surface.

DESIGN

Design your cutouts on the top of the plate and make sure they are in harmony with the shape of your object.

Blu-tack your design to the front of the plate. You must remember, however, that everything will be in reverse. Make certain that any overlaps of the design are in the right order for gluing. The objects in the foreground will be glued to the back of the object first.

GLUING

Only attempt to glue one piece of the design at a time. Select the largest piece first.

1. Hold the cutout comfortably across the splayed fingers of your left hand (if you are right-handed) with the front of the print facing you. Using a soft brush, apply the glue generously all over the face of the print, taking care to push it right to the edges. Smooth out as many bubbles as you can and try to have an even amount of glue all over. At this point, you should not be able to see the colours of your image, just the white film of glue. Ease your fingers to and fro to make sure the image has not become a bit stuck to them.

2. Holding the glass by the edge with your right hand, place the print underneath it in the right position. (Mark the position on the front of the plate with a few bits of blu-tack. This will ensure you place the image correctly underneath.) Turn the plate over and gently tap the image into position with your finger nail.

3. Now hold the plate upright so that the front of the plate is facing you. Hold it with your left hand, keeping your fingers well away from the image and the glue. Dip the middle finger of your right hand in water. Use this finger lightly and, keeping it moist, use it quickly to work out any bubbles. Speed is of the essence (particularly on a hot day) and all bubbles must be cleared before the glue at the edges begins to dry. If you are

working on a large piece of glass and have large areas of cutouts, you may have to cut some escape routes for the air bubbles. These cuts would be made along existing lines of the design so that when they are rejoined, the cuts are not visible.

Keep dipping your finger into water. If it dries, you will move the design out of position or, worse, crinkle it. Find the right touch – it is enough pressure with your wet finger to move the air bubble and not so much that you take glue with it. Pretend you are stroking a butterfly wing.

If any air is left in, there will be a nasty shine on the cutout when it is dried. This shine will also occur if too much glue is pushed out. Don't be deterred if your first attempt ends in a mess. It is a difficult technique, but one you can master. Just wash the whole disaster off, use a fresh cutout and begin again. You will, no doubt, feel like throwing the lot through the nearest window and you won't be the first! Do try again though, for you will succeed.

4. Once the bubbles have been cleared and there is enough glue left under the print, use tissues dampened and rolled into a point, damp cotton buds and sponge pieces to clean up. At this point, concentrate on removing excess glue from around the edges of the design. If the glue has dried near the edges and is difficult to remove, a toothpick will be of help. Once the edges are clear, have a quick clean-up of the rest of the surface, then leave well alone to dry overnight. Further cleaning up will only endanger the design while it is drying. The rest of the excess glue can be removed the next day with warm water. When doing this, keep moisture away from the edges of the design. You don't want to wet the edges of the print and the glue underneath.

5. Sometimes the glue will take longer to dry than anticipated, because of the weather and the type of print. You will know if it has not dried as the glue will still be white. If, after a week, it still hasn't turned clear, pin prick the area to let air in.

6. If there are several parts to your design, glue the next piece in place using the same procedure. Allow each piece to dry before another piece is added.

7. When all the design is in place and the surrounding surface clean and sparkling (a final wipe with vinegar and water will do this), take a small soft brush and seal the back of the prints with polymer medium. If you accidentally brush some on the glass, just clean it off. Leave to dry for several hours.

Now you are ready to paint.

PAINTING

As with all découpage, the painting must harmonise with and complement the design. Some points to remember when painting are as follows:

- Iridescent colours will adhere to the glass. However, they will not 'push through' paint or gesso, so always apply them first.

- Other colours need a small amount of gesso to help them adhere. If you are convinced you need a very dark, almost black, background there is a new product by Liquitex called Glossies, which are paints especially designed to adhere to non-porous surfaces like glass. This paint can also be mixed with Liquitex tube paints. It is not opaque so several layers are needed and beautiful effects can be achieved by using it on top of one of the opalescent paints.

- A brush or sponge may be used to apply the paint, depending on the texture and effect you desire.

METHOD

Hold the plate in your left hand at the edge. With the front of the plate facing you, apply the paint beneath the glass. This way you can see what is happening. Eventually, you will run out of plate for your fingers to hold. Move your middle finger to the back of the largest of the cutouts for it won't matter if the paint is not applied here at this stage. This can sometimes be tricky if there isn't a spot large enough to accommodate your finger. It's helpful at this point to have somebody to hold the plate for you with the edges between their palms. It is only for a moment while you paint that last small area. Without any help, the middle finger on a section of cutout and the plate edge balanced between your thumb and forefinger should hold it.

Holding the edges with your palms, invert the plate on the top of a jar, or similar object, to dry for a day.

When you have finished, the plate should be opaque, so that when you hold it to the light, you cannot see through it. How many layers of paint are needed will depend on how thickly the paint is applied. I give some suggestions for backgrounds below. Paint only one layer each day and allow it to dry thoroughly.

Once the background is opaque, seal the paint with a coat of Estapol lacquer and dry for 24 hours. This ensures that subsequent work on the back of the plate will not disturb your paint in any way. It is now protected, together with the print and glue, from moisture.

SOME BACKGROUNDS FOR UNDER GLASS

PAINTED BACKGROUNDS

You can use any one of, or a combination of, the iridescent colours. Sponge the paint evenly all over the surface and allow to dry thoroughly. Keep repeating this process until it is opaque and you cannot see through the glass.

Apply gesso directly onto small areas and, while it is still wet, push any colour or colours through the gesso to the front. Always look at what you are doing from the front of the glass. If the gesso and paint has dried and left a line by the time you paint an adjoining area, soften it by pressing firmly with a wet sponge. If you absolutely hate the effect, carefully wipe off the paint, taking special care near the cutout edges so you do not wet or disturb them. If you are uncertain about a painted effect, the best way to test it is to try the effect inside a glass jar before tackling your project.

For a soft, shimmering background, apply two coats of iridescent white paint and leave to dry. Mix a little gesso and cobalt blue on your palette (an exception to the general rule) and gently sponge this on. Repeat until background is opaque. You can use any colour this way, so do experiment.

RICE PAPER BACKGROUND

Many, many years ago, I read some instructions in a book from overseas on how to use rice paper behind glass. The beautiful, fibrous effect achieved looked wonderful and I set to with enthusiasm. The instructions mentioned overlapped torn sheets of rice paper (it didn't say what sort) that were glued to the back of a plate. It took me many months to discover that the effect of using this method bore no relation to the photograph that inspired me and I truly hope that nothing in this book makes you feel as mad and as frustrated as I felt about this.

Eventually I managed to work out a method using rice paper. Here it is.

1. Rice paper is sold in sheets at good art shops. It is handmade in Japan and comes in various thicknesses. The fine- or medium-weight paper is best for découpage. It does come in colours, but use white. The paper is soft and has different thickness of fibres in it with no set pattern. These fibres give the effect we are after.

2. The effect is suitable for any form of oriental design, especially if there is movement in it that can be enhanced by the fibres. Other themes can also look interesting backed by the paper.

3. Once the cutouts have been glued, cleaned up and sealed in the usual way, place the plate face up on top of the rice paper so that you are looking at the design. Move the plate about back and forth over the rice paper until you find a pattern in the fibres that complements your design. Draw around the plate in pencil, about an inch clear of the plate edges, and cut the shape out.

4. Place the cut rice paper beside you with the right side facing. Turn the plate over and apply a generous coat of wood glue over the back of the plate so that the whole surface is white. Holding the edges only, place the glued surface of the plate on top of the rice paper. Lift the plate and, keeping your fingers wet, press out the bubbles (but not the glue). Where the plate curves or bends causing a crease in the rice paper, just press the crease down, sticking it with the glue that has seeped through. The crease will look like another fibre on the finished piece. Make sure the edge of the rice paper is stuck well to the edge of the plate. There will be a frill of left-over rice paper all around the plate. Ignore it. Quickly clean off any excess glue that may have seeped through using a damp sponge, but don't be

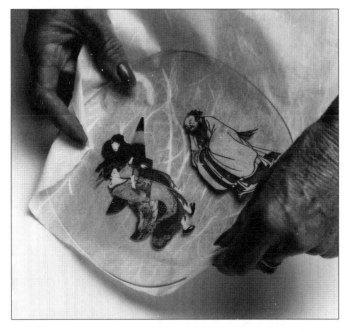

Place the glued surface of the plate on top of the rice paper

overly fussy. Invert the plate over a glass jar, or similar object, and leave it to dry until the glue is perfectly clear.

5. Trim the frill of rice paper sticking out from the edges with scissors so that it is about 3 mm (⅛ in) from the plate edge.

6. Painting is the next step. Flood the paint on to the back so that it is absorbed by the rice paper, but not by the fibres, which form a beautiful rhythmic pattern. It is necessary that the paint is of the right consistency, so add water to the paint to make it flow.

If you have, for example, a Chinese warrior on horseback and you want the fibres of the rice paper to resemble the branches of trees, then select paint to achieve this feeling. Squeeze a little cobalt blue, cadmium yellow medium and a tiny amount of cadmium red medium or scarlet on the palette. Mix a little water with all these colours individually so that they are more liquid than usual. Whether you apply these colours individually or mixed them on the palette (another exception to the general rule) is up to you. Try for a soft but dark, woody feeling. Dark paint is best as the fibres will stand out well. Allow the paint to dry thoroughly. You will be enchanted by the effect.

7. Seal with one coat of lacquer. Dry for 24 hours.

8. The cutout design will be a visible bump under the rice paper, so apply several coats of gesso, then sand. Paint the back a colour to complement the front. Finish in the usual way.

FINISHING THE BACK OF GLASS

Once you have finished painting the background, from the front of the plate you now have a beautiful piece of découpage. The back is a mess. There is paint texture and raised cutouts. The whole of it bears no relation to the front.

What now must be aimed for is a back that is in keeping with the front. If this is done, it is hard to detect how the effect has been achieved. Somebody in my home once picked up a glass plate, rubbed their fingers across the top of the glass in wonder and said: 'Thirty coats of lacquer, eh?' He had no idea that it had been worked from behind.

1. Coat the back with several thick layers of gesso. Allow several hours drying time in between coats. Apply it with a soft brush and work in opposite directions so that you have as few brush marks as possible. This saves sanding time later. The gesso is to build up the level of the surface and disguise the cutouts. Do not have the gesso too thick at the edges of the plate.

2. Sand the gesso until it is smooth with No. 120 stearate sandpaper wrapped around a block.

3. Paint the gesso surface to tone with the design on the front. You may like to paint it a plain iridescent bronze, copper or gold if this is suitable. Allow to dry.

4. Apply half a dozen coats of Estapol, allowing 24 hours drying time between coats. Sand and finish as usual.

5. You are almost there! The front and back now look splendid, but there is still the edge. The edge of the plate will still have untidy remnants of paint, lacquer and gesso or rice paper. Hold the plate firmly against your

Urn with figure in garden

'Cupid', designed with red and silver bands and renaissance paper

OPPOSITE: *Urn divided into panels, bordered with metallic gold bands*

Dancing fairies, toadstools, butterflies and trees on a sunset-painted background

Trays and bowls decorated with the works of Kay Nielsen

OPPOSITE: *Tray with Victorian Christmas theme and Christmas decorations*

Pears behind glass

chest and trim the edges with the type of razor blade that bends. A stanley knife doesn't have any give in it – you need something sharp and flexible. Bend the blade slightly, making sure you are in total control of it, and trim towards you (this is something your mother always said you must never do, so be careful). Trim only a sliver at a time. To finish, you might like to paint the very edge of the plate with iridescent gold, using a 00 brush.

DÉCOUPAGE UNDER AND OVER GLASS

The combination of découpage on both sides of glass gives an unusual three-dimensional effect. It is a lengthy process as both surfaces are worked on, so it is not for the impatient! The example shown in the colour plates is worked as follows:

1. The lady and horse were glued from behind and painted with iridescent gold and copper. The surface was finished in the usual way.

2. The branches and berries were designed on the front of the plate to give the impression that the horse and rider are seen from a distance through the trees.

3. Using a mixture of iridescent gold and cobalt blue, the green was sponged around the edges of the plate and the berries and leaves glued on. The surface was then finished in the usual way and edges trimmed with a flexible blade. A fine layer of gold leaf finished the edges.

CARE OF DÉCOUPAGE

You have put so much work into your découpage, you should treat it carefully.

Never display your work permanently where sunlight filters onto it through glass, or too close to an open fire or heater. It will, however, survive a microwave oven. I often heat soup in a découpage tureen. Do not put it in a convection oven as this may present an uneven temperature. Do not put it in a dishwasher, nor submerge it in water to clean. Just sponge down with warm, soapy water and dry thoroughly.

With vases, unless you have used glass and worked on the outside, it is safest to insert two good quality plastic bags inside the vase and fill them with water. Now you are ready for the flowers. The interiors of fine, antique porcelain vases are often protected this way, and it keeps them dry and free of odour. You need to protect your work from moisture that seeps into tiny cracks that may already be in the glazing. The moisture can travel through to the découpage and damage it.

Découpage, whether it is a finished piece or work in progress, should not be stored in any form of plastic once lacquer has been applied and never leave it in a parked car where the temperature can rise dramatically, even on a winter's day. Lacquer can swell and bubble with the heat.

Take care to place your work safely where it will not fall or be knocked. A fall onto a hard floor can cause:

- a bisque or terracotta piece, or an egg to break, crack or shatter.
- the corner or edge of any wooden box or tray to be damaged.
- the lacquer to be split away from the surface.

REPAIR

If the worst does happen, there are things that you can do.

BREAKAGES AND CRACKS

Stick the pieces with a good-quality china glue. Leave for several days to harden. Sand the repaired area smooth and fill in any missing areas (you may not find all the pieces) with a stiff mixture of polyfilla and PVA glue. When dry, sand this and paint to match. Paint over any cracks and continue to lacquer. Over the years, I have repaired many pieces of work that have been dropped. Students are usually so shattered, they want to hurl it in the nearest bin. It's a great joy to me to show them how to restore both the work and themselves!

CHIPPED CORNERS OR EDGES

Sawdust mixed with PVA glue to a stiff consistency can be applied, a little at a time, to rebuild a corner or an edge. Use a palette knife and be very patient. Let it dry and have another go the next day. Keep fashioning the shape and, when you think it's right, let it set hard for a week. Sand gently with No. 320 sandpaper, then paint, lacquer and sand as usual, concentrating the bulk of the lacquer on the repaired area. A Sydney antique dealer gave me this tip when he happened to be in my studio during such a crisis.

SPLIT LACQUER

Gently sand the area where the lacquer has been chipped – just enough to smooth the edges. Wipe the residue off. In case the chip has gone right down to the cutout, apply one coat of polymer medium to the whole area. Allow to dry. Gradually fill in the area with lacquer. Do not try to do it in one hit for it will take too long to cure and you will have trouble with the final sanding when you come to that area.

Finally, if you are flying, make sure your découpage (either work in progress or any piece finished within the last 12 months) travels in the pressurised cabin with you. The extreme temperature changes in the hold can cause discoloration of the paintwork and the print. This happened to a student's work recently during an hour's flight to Sydney. The work was on a craftwood box and had only had two coats of lacquer. After the flight, some of the colours on the cutouts had suffered a change, causing the soft green shades to turn yellow and brown. There had been a chemical reaction of some sort during the flight. I am still racking my brains as to what happened. Perhaps the formaldehyde content of the craftwood disagreed with the paint or glue when subjected to the conditions of the hold. It is a puzzle. In the early days, when I was still experimenting with lacquers, I used to test them this way. Most cracked under the conditions, but I never saw the paintwork or prints affected. I will find the answer one day, I hope, but meanwhile take your découpage safely in your hand luggage.

Some of the equipment you need to get started

PROJECTS

This section presents a number of projects for you to try. If you have not attempted découpage before, begin with a simple flat oval with an easy to cut and glue design. You will find the lacquering and sanding on this shape is easier as well. A square or oblong piece of craftwood would also be fine. Craft shops have a plentiful supply of shapes.

It is very important to read carefully the instructions in the techniques section before you reach each stage.

EQUIPMENT

Below is a list of the things you will require. Don't fall into a decline! You will not need everything at once. Purchase your needs as you go and you will probably find you have a number of the things already. You may be tackling your first piece with a friend. In this event, share the equipment.

- Fine, curved scissors. The best kind are from a surgical supply house such as Future Medics. Ask for 11.25 cm (4 ½ in) curved iris scissors that are used for eye surgery.
  Other brands include Dova, Lawton 050311, Pfeilring 4234 and Aesculap BC61 or BC5.
- Stanley knife.
  Flexible razor blade.
- 1 can Wattyl Estapol gloss, Cabot's Crystal Clear or Goldspar Epiglass.
- Silicon carbide stearate sandpapers in the following grits:
  No. 120, No. 320, No. 280 (if working with Cabot's) No. 1200 wet and dry.
- Micro-mesh kit or wax polish for finishing.

- SIA Swiss sanding block.
- Lint-free cloth (chamois or new synthetic variety).
- Box of tissues.
- Turpentine (supermarket variety).
- Glass jar.
- Plastic ice-cream lid for palette.
- Tack rag.
- PVA wood glue (Selley's Aquadhere).
- Blu-tack.
- Household sponge.
- Small sea sponge.
- Good quality wallpaper paste.
- Rubber roller.
- Wooden shashlik sticks.
- Brushes (obtainable from art-supply shops):
  1.25 cm (½ in) bristle brush, 1 good quality 2.5 cm (1 in) nylon or sabeline brush, 1 good quality 00 nylon or sabeline brush.
- Jar of Liquitex or Matisse Gloss Medium and Varnish.
- Acrylic paints. See page 27 for the colours and brands that are recommended you buy.

CHRISTMAS NURSERY OVAL

I made this for my granddaughter, Natasha, so that she will have something special of her own for her room each Christmas.

METHOD

1. Sand and bevel the edges of the oval with No 120 sandpaper to smooth the sharp edges of the wood.

2. Measure 2.5 cm (1 in) in from the edges and with a pencil mark a series of dots. Join the dots to form a solid line. Transpose this line to tracing paper then trace onto the back of a sheet of gold wrapping paper. Cut a narrow oval from this paper.

3. Cut out the teddy bears, holly, ribbon and bow. Lay the design on the oval.

4. Now is the time to contemplate colour. I used a muted red behind the bears and phthalocyanine green around the rim.

5. Use a brush, seasponge or a square of household sponge to apply a mixture of crimson and black in the middle. Be careful using the black as it's very dominant. If you get too dark a tone, just apply more red over it and play around with the colours until you get it right. Allow it to dry.

6. Paint pure phthalocyanine green around the outer edge. At this time, don't worry about the side edges or the back. They will become a mess with the lacquer anyway. Also, remember that where the green and red meet doesn't have to be particularly neat as the join line will be covered by the gold paper. Allow to dry for half a day.

7. Glue the gold oval into place with Gloss Medium and Varnish, a little at a time. If you find the paper stretches, cut it at the top so that if the join is uneven, it will be hidden by the bow and holly.

8. Glue the teddies with a thick wallpaper paste, and flatten with a rubber roller. Clean up any excess glue.

9. Using Gloss Medium and Varnish, glue the bow and holly in place. Leave all to dry for two hours.

10. Brush two coats of Gloss Medium and Varnish over the whole to protect the images from lacquer. Allow each coat to dry for one hour.

11. Before lacquering, secure the oval on a glass jar, or similar object, with blu-tack so that it is elevated. This prevents the oval from becoming stuck down to the work surface and allows you to pick up and inspect your lacquering without touching the oval. Be sure that the surface you are lacquering is level.

12. Flood the lacquer on the surface, gently pushing it with the side of the brush, without splaying the bristles. Remember that a warm, breezy day is good for lacquering, so you can add another coat in 24 hours in these conditions. If the weather is still and damp, or just plain humid, leave 48 hours between coats.

13. If the lacquer has been applied thickly enough, you should be ready for a first sand after four coats. Use a block with No. 320 sandpaper wrapped around it and sand very lightly. You are trying to take the lacquer off the images, not the background.

14. After eight or nine coats, you should be ready for the major sand with the No. 320 sandpaper.

15. Clean up the back and sides as you sand. Paint the sides with iridescent gold and the back with phthalocyanine green. Seal these areas with one coat of lacquer.

16. Apply two final thick coats of lacquer to the front and leave to cure for three weeks.

17. Sand off the dust gently, then sand with No. 1200 wet-and-dry sandpaper. Finish with micro-mesh or wax.

18. Fasten a ribbon, or hanging hook, to the back or top of the oval.

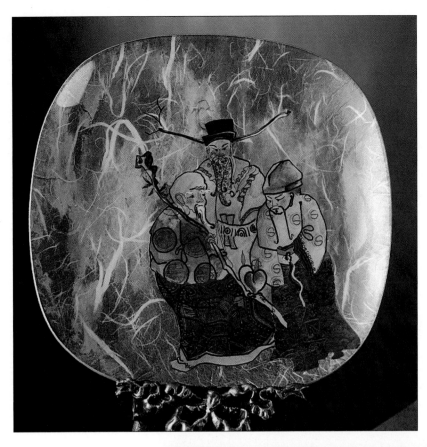

Both the plates illustrated were decorated with découpage from the back, with backgrounds of rice paper

This glass plate was decorated with découpage on both sides to give a three-dimensional effect

OPPOSITE: *Christmas nursery oval*

TOP: *Australian duck*, ABOVE: *Renaissance duck*

DUCKS

If you have ever watched ducks swimming and flying, you will have noticed their beautiful, graceful lines. I like to visualise their quiet progress through the water, so I often design them as if they are swimming, gently dragging leaves and reeds in their wake. I find them friendly birds and thus when people handle a découpage duck, their hands inevitably stroke and caress the fine feel of the finish. It is fascinating to watch students become quite fond of this shape as they work. One said to me, 'Oh, I just love painting his little fat cheeks'.

The two ducks in this section are quite different. The first one has the design lines I have already mentioned, while the second is a richly designed duck, out of his element but proudly bearing his 1600s' design.

AUSTRALIAN DUCK

If you are working on a terracotta duck, seal the inside with some old lacquer for terracotta is very porous. The outside is sealed by your work.

METHOD

1. Paint the duck with a mixture of hookers green and iridescent copper. Work them wet into wet using a soft brush. Work the brush in the direction the feathers would lie. Use some extra copper on the tail and the crest of the head for emphasis.

2. A mixture of iridescent gold and copper is used for the beak. This gives the duck a natural, earthy look that suits the gum leaf design.

3. The eye white is painted with gold, with the iris in hookers green. A fleck of gold applied with the brush tip highlights the eye and brings it to life.

4. Blu-tack the leaves in position, taking care to place them so they follow the shape of the body in an asymmetrical line. Try and imagine the duck's

progress through the water, sweeping the floating gum leaves with him.

5. Glue the leaves a little at a time using Liquitex Gloss Medium and Varnish. Expel any air and excess glue as you go with a dampened piece of sponge.

6. When it is dry, seal your work twice with the Gloss Medium and Varnish. Leave a day before beginning to lacquer.

7. Secure the duck on a jar or bottle with blu-tack so that you can see what you are doing, and can move the duck around without touching it.

8. During the course of lacquering, you will need to watch for drips forming on the cheek, chest and tail area – anywhere where the slope is steep. After applying the lacquer, return in 10 minutes to disperse any drips with a brush moistened in a little turpentine. This will save much sanding later.

9. After six coats or so, sand lightly with No. 320 stearate sandpaper, carefully wiping off the residue with a damp, lint-free cloth. Finally, wipe with a tack rag before lacquering again.

10. Sand about every third or fourth coat of lacquer from now on and when a major sand is reached, you will need to use a sheet of sandpaper folded over to get into the crevices of the shape.

11. Apply two final coats of lacquer. Cure for three weeks and finish with No. 1200 wet-and-dry sandpaper and micro-mesh.

12. Cut a felt shape to fit the base. It should not be too big and, thus, visible under the duck. Draw a template by placing the duck on a sheet of paper and pencilling around the base. The pencil line will give an area much too large, so draw a further line (having first removed the duck) at least 6 mm (¼ in) in from the original line. Cut out this shape and use it as a guide for cutting the felt. I used black felt for both ducks. Use a strong craft glue to adhere it because the felt mostly covers the hole and it has to be held in place at the perimeter.

FLORENTINE -STYLE DUCK

This duck is removed from nature, but it is highly ornamental and very beautiful.

METHOD

1. Paint the shape with mars black. Allow it to dry, then delicately wash over with iridescent copper, emphasising the tail tip, head and beak with iridescent gold and copper. The eyes were painted with copper and gold also.

2. I cut the design from a sheet of wrapping paper that reproduced an early seventeenth-century Florentine tabletop. The paper was printed in Denmark and the original table can be seen in the Rosenborg Castle in Copenhagen. It is not painted, but inlaid with marble, lapis lazuli and other minerals. This gives it a glow of brilliant colours. It is very beautiful and, if you look closely, you will observe the tiny joins where each inlaid piece meets in the pattern.

The shape of this duck is not as slim and sleek as the Australian duck and this allowed for the boldness of the design. The design line is an oval and the largest piece of fruit has been placed at the point where the duck's shape begins to taper. At the time, I felt I had made rather a bold move placing it so far back, but the head and tail appeared to balance it to my eye. The butterfly was placed along the oval line and, although from a different source, they married well. As the design is mainly glued on a curved surface, it had to be cut carefully so there were no wrinkles.

3. Follow all the steps for the Australian duck, including gluing felt to the base.

FAIRY WITCH EGG

Eggs are a delight to work. Pottery eggs are suitable, but there is nothing like working on a real egg. Most cultures have decorated eggs in some form through the ages. Their shapes and sizes vary and some lend themselves to certain uses; for example, a duck egg is an excellent shape for a Christmas decoration. A beautifully decorated egg is a charming wedding or christening gift.

There are three special considerations when working on eggs.

- An egg has a curved shape, which means lots of cutting into the image is necessary to make it fit the curve.
- An egg has a surprising amount of surface area to cover.
- It is quick and easy to lacquer eggs as they can be dipped into the lacquer.

The egg I used here is a large hen's egg and the design is based on Ida Rentoul Outhwaite's fairy witches. Her witches are good witches so that when designing it, I wanted to get a good feeling, not an evil one. I decided to include a spider, a beetle, a twisted tree, a fly, toadstools, a frog and a cat. The twisted tree gave a feeling of wind movement suggested by the witch's garments. I worked the rather murky colours so they lightened towards the top, to give the feeling they were in the open, intent on witch's business!

METHOD

BLOWING THE EGG

An egg blower can be purchased from egg artistry supply shops, but I will assume here that you don't have one and must blow it yourself.

1. Insert a hole in each end of the egg by pushing a darning needle through the shell. The fatter end of the egg becomes the bottom and it is the hole at this end that must be enlarged. Do this by chipping the tiniest piece of shell away with the point of the needle. The secret is to do this a little at a

time. Attempt to remove too large a piece at one time and the shell will crack. The size of this hole needs to be just large enough for the blunt end of a wooden shashlik stick to be inserted, so test for this as you go.

2. Once the hole is the correct size, insert the darning needle gently into the egg and twist it about to break up the yolk. Obviously, if you left the yolk whole, no amount of huffing and puffing would push it through the hole.

3. If you wish to save the contents (being wasteful, I never do) lean over a bowl and place your mouth over the smaller hole at the top. Blow until some of the white comes out. Sometimes it takes a while to get it flowing but once some comes through the bottom hole, the rest follows quite easily.

4. Once you think the egg is emptied, cover the small hole with your finger and hold the large hole under a gently running tap. You will hear a splatter sound as the water pushes through loose membrane. With a couple of tablespoons of water inside, cover the large hole with another finger and give a thorough shake. Blow this out as well.

5. Give the egg a good scrub with a scouring powder to remove any stamped mark and grease spots. Rinse thoroughly.

6. Prop the egg upright on some tissues. Angle it slightly with the large hole at the bottom and allow to drain and dry thoroughly for a few days. It is important that all the moisture is dried for the egg shell is very porous and water must not be trapped inside.

DECORATING THE EGG

1. Cut out the design and blue-tack it on so that you can decide what paint you will use to obtain the mood you wish to set.

2. On this egg I used phthalocyanine green, iridescent copper and gold. These were applied with a small sea-sponge, which gave it a textured feel and added dimension. When painting, the best way to hold the egg is at each end between your forefinger and thumb. This gives a firm hold and makes you feel in charge (which is important). At the ends you will have no paint where your thumb and finger were. To paint these areas, insert

the blunt end of a shashlik stick in the larger hole, pushing it gently up to the top. Hold the stick and paint the missed areas. Poke the sharp end of the stick into a jar of sand or rice and allow the paint to dry for 24 hours. I drill holes in old blocks of wood to hold the stick. You can use whatever you can contrive but do not use florist's foam as it is dissolved by lacquer.

3. Remember that the image must be coaxed to curve by cutting. By holding the witch against the egg and pressing the image gently into place you will form a good idea of where any extra cutting should be.

Use the rules below as your guide when cutting into the design.
- At all costs, avoid faces. Cut around the hair line or chin, but leave the face alone. It is too hard to repair.
- The major cutting will be needed around the widest areas.
- Where possible, cut along an existing line. In this case, the lines between the cape and dress and into her long hair. Also, cut a small nick into the band of the hat.
- It is better to over cut rather than not have enough cuts.

4. Remove the stick from the egg and glue the main images with Liquitex Gloss Medium and Varnish. Gluing needs to be looked at logically. The cape must not overlap the dress, for instance. Place a good quantity of Gloss Medium and Varnish on the egg where the image is to go. Use a 00 brush and gently position the cutout, making sure the right things overlap. When you are happy with the positioning, gently push the image into place with a damp piece of sponge until it is secured. If you have a doubt about an area, invert a brush and use the other end as a miniature roller.

5. Clean up and allow the glue to dry before you proceed to the next cutout.

6. With a curved surface like this, if you work impatiently, your fingers may stick to undried glue at the back of the egg and damage your image. Just wait for each piece of gluing to be touch dry. It is only five to ten minutes.

7. When everything is glued in place and dry, replace the egg on the stick. Stand the stick upright and seal with two coats of Gloss Medium and

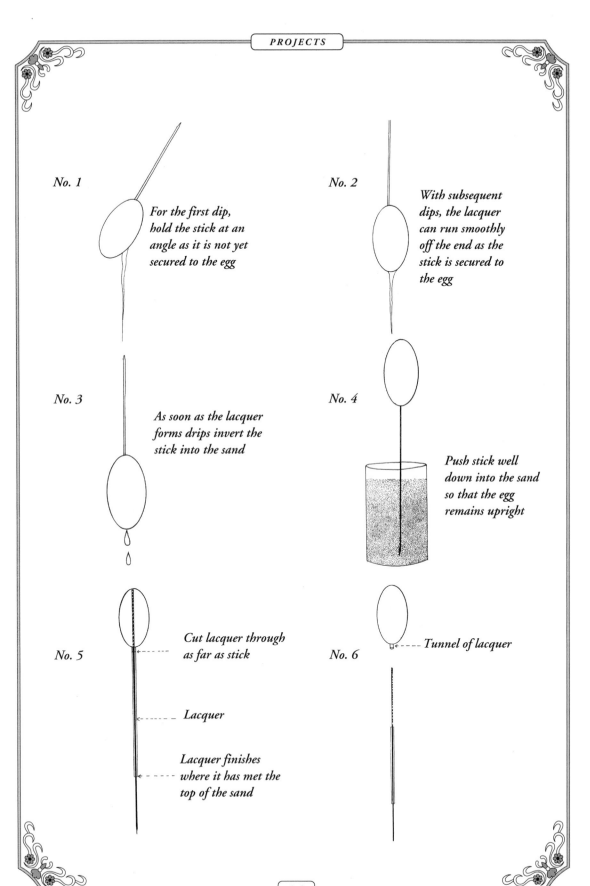

No. 1

For the first dip, hold the stick at an angle as it is not yet secured to the egg

No. 2

With subsequent dips, the lacquer can run smoothly off the end as the stick is secured to the egg

No. 3

As soon as the lacquer forms drips invert the stick into the sand

No. 4

Push stick well down into the sand so that the egg remains upright

No. 5

Cut lacquer through as far as stick

Lacquer

Lacquer finishes where it has met the top of the sand

No. 6

Tunnel of lacquer

Varnish, allowing one hour drying time for each coat. Try and concentrate some of the sealant around the area at the bottom where the stick enters the egg. It will help the bonding of the stick and egg.

LACQUERING

1. If the stick has not bonded to the egg, the first dipping into the tin of lacquer will have to be done with great care. After immersing the egg right into the lacquer, hold the stick at a slight angle so that the lacquer runs off the egg, not at the very end, but at a point towards it.

2. Let all the lacquer run off, but at the very second it ceases to run and begins to drip instead, invert the egg and stand it upright to dry. It is important that you don't let it drip because the lacquer is already beginning to dry and when the stick is inverted, it has to run down the egg in the opposite direction. In fact, it must run the other way onto and down the stick. You should ensure the lacquer is fluid enough to do this or it will stop flowing halfway down the egg and form drips and runs. Therefore, do not dip eggs into old lacquer, which may have thickened.

The first dip adheres the egg to the stick, so subsequent dips are quick and easy.

3. Dip the egg five times before sanding with No. 320 sandpaper on a block. Leave the egg on the stick while doing this.

4. Eight or nine dips, even with design overlap, should be quite sufficient to begin a major sand. It is time to remove the stick. This is done with a sharp, flexible blade. Cut through the lacquer on the stick about 6 mm (¼ in) down from the base of the egg. Do not cut the stick, just the lacquer. When the cut is right around the stick, grasp the egg and twist the stick. The stick will pull out, leaving a small funnel of lacquer. Trim this off with the blade, but not too close to the egg. Let the sanding block take care of the final bit.

5. You will find that dust doesn't settle on the egg during lacquering, so the major sand is just to level the surface of the cutouts and the background. The final dip (which is executed in the same manner as the first dip) will leave a good finish. You may feel the last dip looks so good that

you'll leave it at that. However, I don't care for the plastic look of it and prefer to finish with micro-mesh as usual.

6. Seal off the hole with a tiny cutout that matches the design. Use a strong PVA glue. With a 00 brush, drop a little sealer onto it and when this is dry, repeat the process with lacquer. Allow to dry. The egg is now complete and safely sealed off from moisture.

PHOTOGRAPHS

Old photographs can be wonderfully preserved for ever with découpage. They may be applied to a box, screen, mirror, wooden or bisque oval, table, or any other surface you can think of. If you have only the original photograph, it might be safest to have it copied. I smile as I write this for I am, by nature, dreadfully impatient and have to begin an idea immediately, so have used original photographs in all the projects illustrated.

Colour photographs must be colour photocopied. Something used in the developing process of colour photographs causes a slow chemical reaction when sealed off from air and, over several years, greens fade to sickly yellows and complexions begin to look very strange. The safest of all is to have colour photographs copied in sepia or black and white.

If you are using an original photograph, don't attempt to peel off the back and make it thinner. It is simply not worth the risk. Old photographs can be quite brittle and I prefer not to risk even more recent photographs. It simply means you have to apply a little more lacquer to build up the background, which in turn means that any finer paper used in the design will have more lacquer on it than normal, but I don't mind this. If you mind, copy the photograph on thinner paper.

You will need to use different glues, depending on the photograph you are using.

- For original photographs, brush a thin layer of PVA glue on the back of the photograph and wave it in the air for a few seconds until it becomes tacky. Place it in position on the object and press down with a damp sponge, making sure to clean up thoroughly any glue that has escaped from the edges. If you have the right amount of glue on the photograph and allow it to become tacky enough, there should be none escaping. Place a couple of heavy telephone books on top of the photograph and allow it all to stand for half an hour or so.
- With photocopies, if the photograph is large, use thick wallpaper

paste and a roller; if small, use Gloss Medium and Varnish. Press out excess glue with a damp sponge.

• For the rest of the design, use Gloss Medium and Varnish a little at a time.

You seal off, lacquer, sand and finish the photographs in the usual way.

OVALS

Both these photographs were taken about 1930 and feature family dogs of the time.

The larger oval shows my mother, and I felt it called for a delicate design which would not compete with the subjects. The background paint is three coats dioxine purple with iridescent gold around the outer rim.

The smaller oval is the only informal photograph I have of my grandfather and I chose an art nouveau design to surround it that was strong and suited to the period. The background paint I used was burnt umber and iridescent copper, worked wet into wet together with a rim of iridescent gold.

In both cases, I used PVA glue for the photograph and Liquitex Gloss Medium and Varnish for the flowers and leaves.

THE MIRROR

There was always an ivory-backed mirror of this shape on my mother's dressing table so it was a childhood memory, combined with my own wedding day in 1957, that inspired this mirror. It felt strange to work with an image of myself and my husband but I quashed any misgivings, thinking that in the future a great-grandchild would derive pleasure from it.

I began work on this piece at the weekend and had no access to a colour photocopier. Too impatient to wait, I went ahead with the black and white photographs. The lacquer softened them and I picked up the darker tone on the background at the edge as well.

METHOD

1. The first task is to lay the scrolled design in a pattern to suit the shape of the mirror. The central patterns make natural frames for the faces. Secure them with blu-tack, then take a 4B pencil and carefully outline the scrolls. This is a bit fiddly, but necessary so that you know where to paint the different tones.

2. Remove the cutout design and paint. Have iridescent gold, copper and mars black on your palette. Within the frames use a mixture of all three colours, emphasising the black. In the centre, use just the gold and copper mixed together and rubbed on with a dry brush up to the pencil lines. It will take several layers as iridescent paints are fairly translucent. The edges are painted with all three colours but use less black than within the frame so that the tone is softer. Allow to dry for 24 hours.

3. Use PVA glue on the photographs and glue the scroll design in place with Gloss Medium and Varnish. This is quite a delicate operation so use a 00 brush when gluing and cut the design immediately if you think it may be fighting your direction. The little ovals made up of circles within the design are delicate, but don't worry if you break one – simply push it back into place gently with the brush and continue gluing.

4. Seal thoroughly twice, then begin lacquering. Don't sand until you have applied five very thick coats of lacquer as the highest point will be the photographs if they are the originals, and you should not risk damaging them.

5. When lacquering, only take the lacquer to the top edge of the mirror, leaving the side edges clear of lacquer. Using a turntable will enable you to turn the mirror easily as you go. Concentrate on lacquering around the edge first and then fill in the middle. As it is a flat surface, the lacquer will find its own level as you apply it thickly and it will build up quickly. Lacquer every second day and sand lightly after four coats. Take care around the edges. You'll find a slight rim has formed and it is tempting to sand vigorously here. Don't. A good tip is to sand from the centre outwards – do so very lightly so that the sanding block will just make contact with the raised areas, taking them back.

6. After the final sanding, apply two coats of lacquer and leave to cure as usual.

7. The depth of lacquer over the scrolls (even though there are only two or three coats on the photographs), the subject matter and the way the design appears to be inlaid meant that I didn't want a highly glazed finish. I therefore used only the No. 4000 micro-mesh, sanding in opposite directions, which gave it a silken finish with just the merest hint of a gleam.

8. To finish the front of the mirror, use the same iridescent gold and copper for the middle section of the back. The only design is the family coat of arms on the handle base. This will be a clue in a 100 years' time when someone might wonder who the bride and groom were.

9. Use a 00 brush and paint the upper and lower edges in tones of iridescent gold and copper with black, leaving the wide centre rim bare. Paint this rim with two very smooth coats of gesso, followed by crimson paint. Allow to dry and apply gold leaf as described in the Stoffels' handkerchief box project on pages 99 to 101.

'THE LETTER' URN

The central image is entitled 'The Letter'; it is by an early American painter and was cut from an *Architectural Digest* magazine. I retained the original rose bush background, cutting it so that it was uneven with some of the roses jutted into the background. The accompanying design came from a sheet of wrapping paper in English Chintz Floral Designs, a book of classic gift wraps from the Victoria and Albert Museum in London (published by Portland House and distributed by Crown Publishers Inc., 225 Park Avenue South, New York, New York 10003). For classical découpage, it is a most valuable design resource.

The flowers chosen pick up colours from the main image and their shapes fell naturally into the lines of the urn. I originally had flowers following the image down the sides, but I abandoned that idea in the finished piece. I felt that this led the eye too far down the base. The fine trim around the base of the lid and the knob is metallic gold cut from Christmas-tree icicles.

METHOD

1. For the background; use acra violet, hookers green, iridescent gold and copper. Begin at the base and, working with a slightly damp sea-sponge, pick up a little hookers green, acra violet and copper. Emphasise the hookers green at the base. As you work to the top of the urn, use more acra violet and gold, with only touches of hookers green and copper, so that the top is much lighter. This gives a wonderful depth and glow and sets the image well into the background.

2. To glue the cutouts, I used stiff wallpaper paste and a roller for the main image, Gloss Medium and Varnish – a little at a time – for the flowers and a strong craft glue for the metal trim.

3. Lacquer as for any round object and finish with micro-mesh until a soft, fine porcelain effect is achieved.

4. When you have finished, there will be lacquer dripped under the lid

and onto the base of the urn. Take a stanley knife and carefully remove the drips, working with only a small area at a time. Do not try and remove large areas of lacquer near the edges, but just take a sliver and, if you are not confident, sand it. When it is smooth and neat, paint in a colour to complement the design. Allow to dry and seal with two coats of lacquer before applying the final coat to the rest of the urn.

VENUS URN

This bisque urn was created for a wedding present. The groom was a romantic soul and forever falling in love. Now he was to marry the last and true love of his life, so I thought it fitting to use Venus, the goddess of love. I searched through art books for all the different images of this beautiful, mythical character and found them easily, for she has been a favourite subject of painters, especially during the middle centuries.

METHOD

1. All the images were the right size for the project, except for the main one which was small and cut from a magazine. I had it enlarged when it was colour photocopied. The grapes and twisted vines seemed appropriate for Venus and the cherubs I used on the lid. The twists of the vine made natural frames for the images. I found a border in matching tones for beneath the lid and used a very fine border in metallic gold to finish everything off. The vine was cut to form four gentle arches around the top of the urn, with extra tendrils and grapes coming down to link the central image. Four arches were also used again on the lid.

2. I chose to paint the urn in a deep plum shade, working to a lighter shade towards the base. It gave it a rich, classical feeling, but with a lightness. Place on your palette some acra violet, dioxine purple, iridescent gold and copper. Using a small sea-sponge, all four colours were applied together. More dioxine purple and acra violet were used on the lid and behind the design, while more copper and gold were applied near the base.

3. I used Gloss Medium and Varnish for all the cutouts other than the metallic borders. The tendrils were cut as I glued to coax into the pattern. A strong craft glue was needed for the metal borders. Apply it directly to the metal, but allow a few seconds for it to become slightly tacky before laying it on the shape. Glue 1 cm (½ in) first and wait for it to dry. This will enable you to pull gently the rest of the border as you glue. Cut the

Fairy witch egg

*Photographs
decorating ovals*

Photographs decorating a mirror

The 'Letter' urn

metal where it joins the start of the gluing only when it is all stuck in place. It is difficult to pre-measure it exactly.

4. Seal the surface with two coats of Gloss Medium and Varnish, allowing an hour drying time for each.

5. As I discussed in the Lacquering, page 51, this type of object is best elevated slightly with a lid that is smaller than the base of the urn and secured with blu-tack to a turntable or plate. The urn lid should be blu-tacked to a sauce-bottle top. Apply lacquer generously and quickly around the urn first. The lacquer will form lengthy drips during this stage. Ignore them. As soon as the base is reached, work the brush lightly, but firmly, upwards and then repeat the process downwards. The faster you can work, the better. If you dither and overwork the drying lacquer, you will cause brush marks. This is not a disaster, but it will give you more sanding later and can create grooves that set a pattern for the rest of the lacquering. The lacquer will run off the bottom of the lid and the base of the urn; don't worry about it at this stage as it is cleaned up later. Concentrate on getting the lacquer on with minimum working and fuss. You will know if you are lacquering badly if you see a lot of brush marks when the lacquer dries. Remember not to splay the bristles, but lay on the lacquer with the side of the brush.

6. Sand in the usual way.

7. When the major sand is completed, it is time to clean up the lid and base of the urn. See the instructions on page 91 for how to do this. With this urn I used a mixture of purple, iridescent bronze and copper on the edges.

LAMP BASE

This bisque lamp base was inspired by the Italian Renaissance. The main image of two tranquil girls in a garden, with the lily that is so symbolic of the period, was acquired from a Japanese student. She had been home to Japan for a visit and had brought back an art magazine, which enthralled the class. She held little hope of securing extra copies of the magazine and colour photocopying was not available at the time. When she returned to Japan to live, however, she most kindly tracked down a back issue of the magazine and sent it to me, so I wanted to produce something special with one of the images.

As the magazine was in Japanese, I have no idea of the painter's name but could recognise the period because of its distinctive style. I then had to find some other authentic resources. I cut the smaller images from a book on Italian Renaissance illuminations by J.J.G. Alexander (published by Chatto & Windus in 1977) and used a fine Florentine paper for the rest. This just left the problem of the arches that I wanted on the upper part of the base and the top. Not being able to find any of the size I needed, I cut my own and painted them using a mixture of crimson, cadmium red and iridescent gold, dirtying them slightly with a delicate wash of ultramarine blue and dioxine purple. The central image was cut in a medallion shape to keep the feeling of the theme.

METHOD

1. The colours of the Renaissance are quite distinctive due to the pigments that were used, and the problem confronting me was not only to match the colours, but to take into account that the colour would change with the coats of lacquer. Last year, when Dr Romano Toppan was here from the Art Institute in Venice, he became highly excited and said the restorers in Italy would kill to achieve such authentic colouring. I offered to write out exactly what I'd used, but his interest waned when he realised I'd used

Liquitex acrylics. There is just no use puzzling over this aversion to modern materials, as I have mentioned before, they are locked into traditional materials and techniques.

Pencil a line where the two tones are to meet. The green palette was made up of cerulean blue, cadmium red medium, cadmium yellow medium and iridescent bronze. The blue, red and yellow were worked into each other, using a greater quantity of the blue. When dry, a fine glaze of bronze was applied over it. It was worked with a soft brush, quickly and gently in a circular motion so that no brush marks were evident.

The red palette was made up of mars black, crimson, cadmium red medium, acra violet and iridescent gold and copper. A plain black background was applied to the area that is deep red and allowed to dry for 24 hours. Using the same soft brush, all of the other colours were worked together over the black until a soft gentle glow was achieved – the colour suggesting a mellow brick.

The cutout borders masked where these two colours join.

2. The images are all different but the Florentine design is repeated in an orderly fashion. This meant quite a lot of measuring (and cursing and swearing) but be assured, it's worth it in the end! The medallion is lower than I normally would like, but the rest of the design dictated its position. I was happy to discover the two cream butterflies. The lower one was used to mask an area where the medallion edge didn't meet evenly and the top one I incorporated into the landscape on the left to balance.

The three top sections and the base carry the heavy design, leaving the central image free and uncluttered, with only a diamond-shaped Florentine pattern placed on the same level beneath each arch.

Six very fine, gold metal borders were the final touches; these suggest gold leaf, which was always a part of illumination work.

3. When gluing, I used Liquitex Gloss Medium and Varnish, applied a little at a time, for the Florentine design and thick wallpaper paste for the central image. As with all metals, I used a strong craft glue for the gold borders.

The arches and oval medallions were glued first so that I could position the main medallion correctly. It is not easy, even with lots of cutting, to stick a medallion this shape and size on a curved surface without getting an uneven edge. I almost managed, but there was the slightest overlap on the lower right-hand side. As it was the only copy of the picture I had, I didn't want to risk lifting it and trying again, but used the butterfly to disguise it instead. I think it must have been successful for no-one has ever noticed it, so well do the butterflies merge with the whole.

4. It was sealed, lacquered, sanded and polished as usual. Don't be like me and take for ever to buy a brass fitting and shade for your lamp!

STOFFELS' HANDKERCHIEF BOX

Years ago, Stoffels packaged their handkerchiefs in delightful little boxes. I suppose that, having decided to preserve one of these boxes, I should have selected a Swiss design for it. However, I decided to use a wrapping paper – one that I collected long ago. With hindsight, I should have bought dozens of sheets of this particular paper at the time, for it is delightful and the paper is now out of print.

The design is taken from a tall sixteenth-century cabinet in the Palazzo Vecchio in Florence. Having often worked with the design, I was very keen to view the cabinet last year when I was in Florence. I dragged my long-suffering companions through room after room searching for it. Beautiful though this tall, magnificent, inlaid cabinet is, I feel my friends were unprepared for my reverence for it. After all, I knew every tiny little piece of the design intimately and was thrilled to see its magnificence at close hand. Looking at the fine, painstaking workmanship was a humbling experience.

Although this paper is no longer available, there are many beautiful designs around that you could use to achieve a similar effect.

METHOD

1. When I was designing this piece, the urn of flowers looked splendid on the lid, but I still cut and re-arranged the flowers to suit my shape. Tiny pieces were placed in the corners and the edges were given a narrow trim. Along the side of the lid, flowers and leaves were cut individually and arranged to fit the narrow space. The front piece has two birds taken from a different source facing each other, they are linked with the same flowers as in the border.

2. Three coats of dioxine purple paint was the base. The lacquer turns this to a very dark navy that is almost black. It was important to have a complementary background, but one that did not compete with the design.

3. Remember that when lacquering a box, it is far quicker to lacquer only the upright surface. Return in an hour or two and turn the box on its side, then apply lacquer to the upper most surface. Continue until all the surfaces have been lacquered. This will avoid drips and allows the lacquer to be applied more thickly.

4. As a final touch, I covered the interior of the box with gold leaf, which gives it a magnificent glow. This is a painstaking process and rather expensive. If you shudder at the thought of it, just paint the inside with iridescent gold and copper paint. For those of you who would like to try gilding, read on.

To gild you will need:
- book of gold leaf (available at good craft stores)
- bottle of Japan Gold size
- two soft, flat brushes
- shellac.

You also need a very smooth surface upon which to work. Sand any imperfections and, if the surface is bad, apply two or three coats of gesso and sand again until it is smooth and silky. Paint with a base colour. I like to use deep red, but other primary colours can be used and will give a slightly different effect. The gold leaf mainly covers the paint, but just a few specks may be visible here and there.

My advice is not to attempt to work too large an area at time. Brush some size thinly on the bottom of the box and leave it for ten minutes or so until it is tacky.

The most tricky aspect is handling the gold leaf because of it delicacy. It comes in gossamer-fine sheets between leaves of tissue. To cut gold leaf, cut through both it and the tissue sheets together. I prefer to pull it into pieces. To do this, flick a soft brush back and forth through your hair at the back of your neck, this creates static electricity to which the gold leaf can cling. Expose an area of gold leaf and, while still holding half of the leaf, between the tissue sheets, allow a small area to attach itself to the brush. Pull the brush gently and a portion of the gold leaf will be separated from the main sheet. Carry this very carefully to the tacky area of the surface and lay it down gently. Stroke it into place with the softest possible touch of the brush. Repeat the process, overlapping the gold leaf on the previously laid gold leaf. Once it is dried (this will take one to three days) remove the excess with a clean, soft brush.

Finally, apply a coat of shellac with a brush to preserve it.

This is a fiddly process and, no doubt, a master craftsman would be shocked by this technique. However, for découpage it works well and it looks old and a bit worn, which goes well with découpage. So steel yourself to waste some of the precious metal and don't despair if your first efforts are a bit of a mess.

SOAPS

Soaps are wonderful to decorate, they are a touch of fun and make charming presents. Strictly speaking, they are not découpage as they only have two or three light coats of lacquer, but why go to all the trouble of sanding and finishing something that will be used up in the bathroom? Nonetheless they should be beautifully painted and designed. Tilly's, in Australia, make ideal round and oval soaps, which are so much more interesting than the usual oblong variety.

One Christmas I designed soaps for all the men in my life with cutouts that pertained to their profession or favourite sport. Another year, I did everyone's dog or favourite animal. Remember that they must have instant appeal, so choose a sharp, bright image and use strong Christmas colours for the paint.

METHOD

1. One week before commencing work on the soap, cover the smooth top half with a couple of coats of Estapol lacquer. This will protect your design from moisture as the soap is used for, of course, the Estapol is oil based.

2. Cut out the design, place it on the soap and consider the background colour. I used phthalolyanine green as the background for the little angel and holly, the holly leaves being a light enough green not to be lost. The Christmas look was enhanced by a band of red painted around the rim, edged with iridescent gold dots applied with a 00 brush. The background to the dogs is a mixture of burnt umber, iridescent gold and cerulean blue that complements the colour of the central image. A thin gold band around the edge was the finishing touch.

3. When the paint is dry, glue on the images. As the soap is slightly curved, you will need to cut the images.

4. Seal with Liquitex Gloss Medium and Varnish.

5. Apply three to four coats of lacquer. I cannot resist a small, light sand

before applying a final coat. It's worth it, for it makes quite a difference to the final look.

6. Don't worry about any drips of lacquer and paint on the underneath side of the soap. When you have finished, remove them with a fine razor blade. Don't gouge into the soap – a delicate touch with the blade is needed.

7. Leave to cure and harden for a week before packaging the soaps in little cellophane bags. Tie the bag with a matching ribbon to make a delightful gift.

VICTORIAN LETTER HOLDER

My husband made this Victorian letter holder for me from a drawing I made. Not being a carpenter and having few tools to hand, it took some time to hand cut it from 5 ply marine plywood. I was overjoyed with it for I already had pansies in my mind to decorate it, and it was to be a gift for a dear friend on a special occasion. This friend's magnificent cottage garden is filled with all the treasured and often-forgotten flowers of the past, and pansies are one of her special loves.

The outdoor, sunlit, tea-time scene seemed to be in keeping and picked up the tones of the pansies. The moths and butterflies I extracted from a book on the history of insects and the pansies were from a magazine specialising in Victorian themes. The front and back panels were worked separately and joined together when finished.

I had envisaged it hanging in my friend's kitchen, crammed with mail. However, no matter what I say, it hangs in the living room in the company of her exquisite antique furniture and, no doubt, will never even sight a postage stamp.

METHOD

1. The background was painted with a mixture of hookers green, iridescent gold and copper, all worked wet into wet. This set the garden feeling. I didn't use too much gold for the sunshine because, although I wanted a slightly, textured look, I didn't want the background to compete with the images. I used iridescent copper around all the side edges.

2. Four holes were drilled in the back and two on the front before work was commenced. The design was actually glued over these and the holes re-opened by poking a shashlik stick through them. It was inevitable that lacquer would trickle into them, so before the final finish, the lacquer was removed with a hand drill. Before drilling, another board was secured over the lacquered surface to hold the lacquer firmly down as the the drill bit

went through. If you do not do this, there is a risk the lacquer will be lifted from the surface.

3. Glue, seal, lacquer, sand and finish in the usual way.

4. All the edges of the letter holder were bevelled so that they are slightly rounded. They were smoothed with No. 120 sandpaper.

5. The two boards of the letter holder are hinged at the base with a strip of book-binding material, as I had seen done on an original Victorian letter holder. The strip is cut 10 cm (4 in) wide and then folded in half. One half is glued with craft glue to each board. This then acts as a hinge and prevents the letters falling through.

6. Two pieces of fine, silken, green rope were threaded through the holes and knotted, a touch of craft glue on the knot will prevent them unwinding with use. The rope on the back board is to hang the holder on a wall. The other rope holds the front board slightly open to receive letters. By pulling that rope from the back, the panel can be closed and made flush with the backboard.

RENAISSANCE VASE

With hair down to her knees and a coiffure that is as fascinatingly elaborate as her bodice, I could not resist working with this delicately posed lady holding a lidded drinking vessel. The oblong shape of the painting so suited the shape of a tall vase that I left it intact. I thought that an elaborate, wrought iron type of design would suit the picture well. Many years ago, I had a wrapping paper with just the design I envisaged. Alas, when I located it, most had been used on other works. I overcame this by photocopying parts of the pattern repeatedly, then painting it after cutting the shapes out. Even the original paper had to be painted a dull metal colour, as it was a rather hectic mustard shade.

METHOD

1. The first task was to shape each end of the image into an oval. This gave it a more gentle look and, more important, counteracted the narrowing shape of the vase at the base. I did not have anything suitable, so I drew some designs, cut them out, then painted them a dull gold colour (a mixture of iridescent copper, gold and black paint). Next the borders were positioned; I linked the curves above and below the image with two narrow Gothic arches on each side. This still left the problem of the curves seeming to be too wide at the bottom. Wider Gothic arches around the

A photocopy of the only part of the original paper that I had left;
this was painted after it had been cut out

106

'Venus' urn

Lamp base

Stoffels' handkerchief box

ABOVE & OPPOSITE: *Renaissance vase*

BOTH PAGES: 18th century Chinese screen

LEFT: *Soaps*

BELOW: *Victorian letter holder*

central image managed to counter-balance these, together with having the lower sections at a slight angle.

A flower paper acquired in Florence last year was ideal to wind in and out of the arches. The only difficulty was that some of the pattern was in a strong aqua colour. This was promptly painted dull gold, which had a softening effect on the whole and the pink flowers alone carried the theme through the whole vase.

The birds and butterflies were from other resources, but the bees on the top curve were from my original paper and fortunately, enough were left to allow them to be repeated. Their off-white wings picked up the tonings in the sleeve and dress yoke on the main image. It is interesting to note that no two bees were identical, but all fitted in the circles.

Finally, I was left with the area under the top lip. A design had to be fashioned and cut for this as I just couldn't find anything to use. The border under the lip was made from inter-linking sections cut from the large circles.

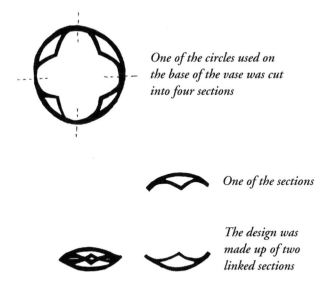

One of the circles used on the base of the vase was cut into four sections

One of the sections

The design was made up of two linked sections

I looked so hard and so long at this project that, in the end, I wasn't even sure I liked it. Done primarily to illustrate how to cope with an over-all design using straight lines on an object that was shaped from wide to narrow, I couldn't help but wonder just how differently I might have designed it, if left to my own devices. It was rather like designing a commission. Somehow the *joie de vivre* goes out of creating once limitations and deadlines are set.

2. Aside from the main image, for which I used wallpaper paste and a roller, this all was glued with Liquitex Gloss Medium and Varnish. It was also sealed with two coats of the same.

3. Estapol was applied liberally in a circular fashion around the vase, which had been secured on a turntable, and then the brush was dragged lightly and quickly up and then down. Since the vase is tapered, I found it easiest to insert my left hand into the top and hold it at an angle for the downwards stroke. Take great care around the handle area to avoid drips.

4. Sanding and finishing were executed as usual.

5. The top section of the inside was painted with gesso, sealed off with lacquer and then painted with the same dull gold colour used in the design (a mixture of copper, gold and black). This area and the handles were left unlacquered.

EIGHTEENTH-CENTURY CHINESE SCREEN

The first student who said to me, 'Hello, I just want to learn a little about découpage so that I can do a screen. Can I do one this term?' caused me to reel in shock. I now just smile warm encouragement and make meaningless, vague mutterings, quite safe in the knowledge that by the third or fourth lesson their ambition will be put on the back burner for a while. They are never disappointed that they cannot produce a screen instantly – they are simply too busy planning all the smaller and more manageable projects that fill their heads.

The sheer dimension of a screen does require developed skills in painting and design, not to mention the technical aspects despite the fact that it is a flat surface (the easiest on which to work). As I write this, a group of advanced students is working to produce an exhibition of screens. It is a four-year project and we are already two years into it. It takes months for an artist to develop a concept and then find the necessary resources. One student has taken all year just to cut out her very complicated border. The theme of her screen is Camelot and it will capture the essence of this legendary place because she has given so much time and effort to her research and design. Another student is a musician who is working on the theme of Strauss. Others are based on the four seasons in Art-nouveau style, Georgian reflections; the Byzantine period; Australian themes, and so on. They are all very different and reflect the devotion and work of each artist. It is special to be associated with such a project and the progress of the screens is extraordinarily exciting to observe. These screens are all sizes, shapes and styles. Some are made from craftwood and others from 5 ply marine plywood. One is being worked on glass, while another is an antique shape. If you are tackling your first screen, choose a small triptych, or a summer screen for the fireplace, before working on a full-sized four-panel one.

A visit to China inspired the theme for this 1.8 m (6 ft), four-panelled screen. I was saddened that the colour and richness associated with pre-revolutionary China seemed to have disappeared, but was comforted by the fact that the flora and fauna was unchanged. It was this I tried to express. It took some time to collect the images that were eighteenth-century, and then many months to cut them out. A friend made the panels for me from 5 ply marine plywood and they are hinged with removable pins so the panels can be wrapped and transported separately any time the screen has to be moved.

The whole screen took a year to complete, but I do not regret a single moment spent on it.

METHOD

1. The design had to flow right across the four panels. The bright areas of red had to be balanced across the whole. The gentle arches in the design reflect the top of the panels. The bamboo near the duck in the left-hand corner needed to be coaxed to meet the smaller peacock, which was in identical tones. The trees and branches on the right had to be joined and manipulated to flow correctly also. I set mother-of-pearl into some of the larger flowers. In the end, I felt nothing demanded your attention but the eye wanders to the magnificent central peacock that I was fortunate to find in the southern provinces of China.

2. To paint the background, I set the four panels upright, side by side in the studio so that they formed a huge canvas. Painting was a huge challenge to me. I knew the feeling I wanted to convey, but just how to get it took some considerable forethought. Being sure before beginning was vital for, as any artist knows, over-painting kills the spontaneity. I wanted to capture China in the early morning mist, with the sun just coming through and the merest hint of mountains.

3. The colours I used on the palette were cobalt blue, titanium white, crimson, burnt sienna and iridescent white. Using a large sea sponge, cobalt blue and titanium white were worked together, patting and dragging in a slow, arched movement. While still wet, a hint of crimson was added to give the softest of blushes. The mountain areas are a combination

of cobalt blue, burnt sienna and crimson. When it was completely dry, a substantial covering of iridescent white was sponged over. It is this that gives the sparkle and life to the whole. The yellow content of the lacquer turns it all to a warm, cream colour but because I used fresh Estapol, the blues were not lost.

4. When the gluing was completed, I used mother-of-pearl flakes to enhance some of the flowers. I have not found a source in Australia for these flakes, but they are available from craft shops in America. Some craft shops here stock mother-of-pearl dust, similar to glitter dust, so you could experiment with this. Put PVA glue on the flowers and lay the flakes over this, pushing them gently with the wooden end of the brush. The flakes may be cut to shape, in which case, soak them for several hours in warm water before cutting so they are not so brittle. The pieces vary greatly in shape and size, so if you spread them out on a sheet of paper, you will probably find the shape you are looking for. Don't try and clean off the glue, it will dry clear. When it has dried, you will find small areas you have missed, so just repeat the process and fill in the gaps. It is hard to see clearly at first because of the white glue. The mother-of-pearl will not be raised once you have sanded in the usual way. Don't worry if you sand back to the mother-of-pearl as it retains its appearance and doesn't become white like the cutouts. I have often used mother-of-pearl for a duck's bill, or to give a gleam to part of a costume. It adds a beautiful lustre.

5. I actually lacquered these panels outside, balancing them on a table. Needless to say, the odd dragonfly and bee met a sticky end (don't remove them until the lacquer has dried). Do the final coats of lacquer inside. With such an area to sand, I tried using a machine sander, but it was too heavy and, surprisingly, took too long. Because of its weight, I found it kept sanding the lacquer off the background instead of the images alone. The Swiss block and stearate sandpaper remained the quickest method.

CONCLUSION

I hope that all this knowledge I have gained over so many years will serve as a guide and inspiration to all découpeurs. It is such a joyful and rewarding art form – the pitfalls can be remedied easily.

There are a few added decorative touches with which you can happily experiment. I have described using mother-of-pearl on the screen and gold leaf on the Stoffels' handkerchief box, but have neglected to mention an illumination effect you may like to use. Just glue a small piece of silver or gold foil to the painted surface and place your cutout over that. The foil gleams through the cutout areas and can be very effective. There are just endless possibilities and each one of you will come up with something of which I never dreamed. It is this that makes découpage so exciting, fulfilling and totally individual.

Try hard not to get lost in the technicalities of the art. Traditional methods have been followed but streamlined with modern paints, abrasives and lacquers. The researchers among you will come up with different and more efficient products as technology progresses. However, as you experiment, make sure that these products of the future don't take anything away from the beautiful glow and tactile surface of your découpage.

GLOSSARY

Acrylic
Water-based paints or lacquers

Bevel
Reducing a square edge to a sloping edge

Bisque
Unglazed white porous porcelain

Blu-Tack
A plasticine-type material that adheres paper temporarily to surfaces

Découpeur
One who practises découpage

Estapol
Brand name of an oil-based polyurethene lacquer or varnish

Florentine
Relating to Florence, Italy

Gesso
A thickly chalky liquid made from gypsum and glue used for disguising imperfections in materials, hardening materials (such as styrene foam) and building up behind glass

Gilding
Laying layers of gold leaf to a surface. The term can also be used to refer to highlighting handles and rims with gold paint

Glaze
A thin topcoat of transparent paint

Grit
The grade of sandpaper. # = the sign for grit

Impasto
Process of laying on paint thickly

Opaque
Impenetrable, solid colour

Palette
A surface on which to place paints. Also refers to the range of colours placed on that surface

Polymer Medium
A water-based white fluid which dries clear and is used as a sealant or a glue. Also known as 'Gloss Medium and Varnish'

Primary Colours
Red, blue, yellow

Renaissance
The culture and style of art between the 14th and 16th centuries

Shellac
A traditional lacquer

Stanley Knife
A razor blade held in metal or plastic – a craft knife

Tack Cloth
A sticky cloth to remove dust

Template
Copy of a pattern usually made with paper or cardboard

Terracotta
Orange/brown coloured earthenware – very porous

Tonal
Harmony of colours

SUPPLIERS

New South Wales

Beverley Currie
Egg Artistry Supplies
3 Hazel Place
Cronulla 2230
Ph: (02) 523 4540

Janet's Art Supplies
145 Victoria Ave
Chatswood 2067
Ph: (02) 417 6048

Lugarno Craft Cottage
243 Belmore Rd
Riverwood 2210
Fax: (02) 533 1485
Ph: (02) 584 1944

Penbrook Cottage
45 Moulder St.
Orange 2800
Ph: (063) 62 0461

Western Australia

Arts & Crafts Corner
34 Mint St.
East Victoria Park 6101
Ph: (09) 361 4567

The Craft House
210 Nicholson Rd
Subiaco 6008
Ph: (09) 381 2880

South Australia

Gaby's Craft Centre
26 Renaissance Arcade
Adelaide 5000
Ph: (08) 223 2984

Cottage Rose Gifts and
Crafts
514 Goodwood Rd
Daw Park 5041
Ph: (08) 2710100

Queensland

Crafts Galore
Shop 1A, Peninsular Fair
Kippa-Ring 4020
Ph: (07) 284 3463

Eckersley's
91-93 Edward St
Brisbane 4000
Ph: (07) 221 4866

Oxlades Art Store
136 Wickham St
Fortitude Valley 4006
Ph: (07) 252 8238

The Craft Crowd
Shop 60, Sunnybank Plaza
Main Rd
Sunnybank 4109
Ph: (07) 345 9812

Tasmania

Interior Dressups
122A Elizabeth St.
Hobart 7000
Ph: (002) 34 5469

Marshiles Craft Centre
22 Stewart St
Devonport 7310
Ph: (004) 24 6171

Victoria

Handworks Supplies
121 Commercial Rd
Prahan 3181
Ph: (03) 820 8399
Fax: (03) 820 8312

Paper'n'Things
88 Union St
Armadale 3143
Fax: (03) 822 2783
Ph: (03) 576 0223

Romantique Haberdashery
68 Milton Parade
Malvern 3144
Ph: (03) 822 5293

The VADA Shop
369 Camberwell Rd
Camberwell 3124
Ph: (03) 882 7082

Tilley Soaps Pty Ltd
29 Clarice Rd
Box Hill South 3128
Ph: (03) 898 7301
Fax: (03) 890 1644

INDEX

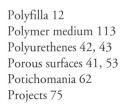